MW00893441

TWO ROADS DIVERGED AND I TOOK BOTH

MEANINGFUL WRITING INSTRUCTION IN AN AGE OF TESTING

MELANIE MAYER

authorHOUSE®

AuthorHouse™
1663 Liberty Drive
Bloomington, IN 47403
www.authorhouse.com
Phone: 1-800-839-8640

First published by AuthorHouse 6/17/2010

ISBN: 978-1-4520-2866-8 (e)
ISBN: 978-1-4520-2864-4 (sc)
ISBN: 978-1-4520-2865-1 (hc)

Library of Congress Control Number: 2010907894

Printed in the United States of America
Bloomington, Indiana

This book is printed on acid-free paper.

To my mom,
Jean Mayer,
who introduced me to books,
and always believed I would write one.

CONTENTS

Introduction: The False Dilemma xi

Chapter One: The Reading-Writing Connection 1

Chapter Two: Writing as a Social Act 29

Chapter Three: The Grammar Connection 47

Chapter Four: Politics 65

Chapter Five: Assessment 95

Conclusion: The Difference 111

Works Cited 116

"The Road Not Taken"
By Robert Frost

Two roads diverged in a yellow wood,
And sorry I could not travel both
And be one traveler, long I stood
And looked down one as far as I could
To where it bent in the undergrowth;

Then took the other, as just as fair,
And having perhaps the better claim,
Because it was grassy and wanted wear;
Though as for that, the passing there
Had worn them really about the same,

And both that morning equally lay
In leaves no step had trodden black.
Oh, I kept the first for another day!
Yet knowing how way leads on to way,
I doubted if I should ever come back.

I shall be telling this with a sigh
Somewhere ages and ages hence:
Two roads diverged in a wood, and I-
I took the one less traveled by,
And that has made all the difference.

INTRODUCTION

The False Dilemma

"I have recognized the limits of my knowing."
-Virginia Crisco

AFTER TWENTY YEARS IN THE CLASSROOM, I recently returned to graduate school. And it wasn't by choice. It was to satisfy the "powers that be" at the college where I adjunct, that I am "current" on issues of basic writing. Apparently my Masters Degree, earned decades before, was insufficient. I was a reluctant student, to say the least; having taught all levels of high school English, from technical writing to advanced placement, with much success for twenty years, I felt more than qualified to teach college freshmen. But I lacked a specific course designation on my transcript: teaching basic writing. So, grudgingly and grumpily, I acquiesced.

I almost quit the first night, when I walked in and saw the weird table with built-in computers under hoods that I didn't know how to work, and listened to the initial philosophizing of my classmates, younger than I by two decades: "bad grammar doesn't mean someone is a bad writer;" "some students are just on the periphery of a diverse learning culture" (huh??); and "grades are the oppressive tools of a dominant society" (seriously?). The instructor was younger than I, and apparently the new grading system in graduate school involved the use of a "check." By the second class it became obvious I would need a tutorial, in order to post responses to weekly readings on the "wiki" (what?) so my classmates could simultaneously refute, attack, and contradict my "old school" thinking. Heaven help me. Couldn't I just type something and turn it in for a letter grade?

My young classmates in "ENGL 5361: Basic Writing Theory and Pedagogy" focused discussions of the readings on theory, culture, and politics. But my concern was always pragmatic. I teach six different high school classes every day, to all levels of students, and freshman composition at the local community college part time. I wanted solid research that would inform my writing instruction, particularly in this age of testing and technology. My experience as an adjunct professor at the college has shown me that most incoming freshmen are indeed barely adequate writers, yet as a high school teacher, I know we are teaching writing. Being in both camps yields an interesting perspective: as a high school English teacher, I must prepare students to master curriculum driven assessments in areas of vocabulary, grammar, reading comprehension, and timed writing assessments; as a college professor, I am appalled at the shallow, boring, unorganized, and stylistically and grammatically incorrect writing I receive from freshman composition students. Somewhere along the way, in our attempts to meet the demands and pressures on us as teachers and the current generation of students, something good has been lost and must be reclaimed. Likewise, in this digital era of increased technology, gadgets, and entertainment, something new must be found with which to instruct and inspire. A balance must be struck between writing for tests and writing for meaning; between method and motivation; indeed, between beauty and the beast. Perhaps we as teachers, and consequently, our students, could benefit from some practical application of the current research about writing instruction.

The National Commission on Writing for America's Families, Schools, and Colleges agrees. Established in 2002 by the College Board to reform the teaching of writing, the commission, including teachers, university presidents and chancellors, writing program directors, school superintendents, authors, the president of the College Board, deans and classroom teachers, and researchers, released the last of four reports in 2006. The first report acknowledged the "need for a writing revolution," in a title by the same name, citing "that it is not that students cannot write but that they cannot write well" (VanDeweghe). This, according to many college professors, is the problem. The final report was blunt: "Standards have turned into standardization. Accountability has emphasized what will be tested, not what should be learned." This may well be the cause of the problem. Classroom teachers know these statements are true; they just don't know quite what to do about it. Indeed, as the pressure to get the lowest level of students to write well enough to pass timed assessments has increased, the tests have become the standard by which we base writing instruction, and ability. In our efforts not to leave a child behind, we leave many others unchallenged, unmotivated, and unprepared for greater goals than the test. We end up dropping the ball for those students who would be writers – who would take risks, break rules, and move us to laughter and tears, if we'd give them a little motivation, opportunity, and access. We limit our students by focusing on a standard. Particularly in an age of testing, where everything is judged by a rubric, the challenge for teachers is to inspire students, not merely inform them. But inspiration takes time, and those tests are always looming. Most of our students have the same mentality: if you ask them what their purpose is in reading something assigned in class, they will likely say, "We are going to have a quiz." And if you ask them why they are revising, and rewriting, they will say, "We have to turn in a draft." We as English teachers want more students to fall in love with books and writing, to anticipate and not dread writing assignments. We want them to "get it," to be so inspired by our classes that they themselves become writers. And so, I reasoned that this course in basic writing instruction, at the very least, would provide access to the research and conversations with other professionals interested in writing pedagogy. The more I learned, the more I could help my own students make meaning and have more authentic experiences in the writing classroom and beyond.

One of the biggest obstacles facing English teachers is the illusion of polarization within areas of the field. We believe, for some reason, that we have to choose a position: emphasize correctness or rhetorical choice; reading class or writing class; academic or personal writing; error analysis or skill and drill; theory or practice; meaning or accountability; the test or the soul. Why do we see the roads as so divergent? What if there were practices that connected instead of isolated the many components of writing instruction? In fact, the research is all about connections. It is teachers' lack of knowledge of the research, uncertainty about how to implement it, hesitancy to try something new, or pressures of curriculum and assessment, that lead us to teach the way we always have, or worse, to teach the content and minimum skills we know will safely enable students to *at least* pass the assessment. We inadvertently perpetuate the false dilemma! Thus, our students still fail to see grammatical correctness as a useful conduit through which they may accomplish communicative purposes, rather than an isolated component of English Language Arts. We still teach reading (The test! The test's to blame!) for summative recall and information, and not for appreciation, awe, and study of the language. We bemoan our struggles with accommodations, mainstreaming, and language learners without realizing there are techniques that provide greater access, and thus a fuller, richer academic and writing life, for these basic writers. Our own assessments start to mirror those of the state or colleges; we even call them "practice tests" or "benchmarks". After my own exposure to and application of research and theory in my classroom, I realized the way I had always approached writing instruction and assessment, was not necessarily the very best way for all students. In fact, I discovered many research-based theories and ideas to which I, though a writer, a veteran composition teacher and English department chair, had never been exposed, and which, when integrated into a classroom teacher's current writing instruction, can make a huge difference in student motivation, access, and outcome. We as teachers can empower ourselves to inspire and instruct students through connecting and not isolating these curricular components, and connecting the writing they do in the classroom to their lives beyond the classroom. And when meaningful instruction is happening, successful testing – and smooth transition between high school and college writing classes - becomes a by-product.

I want to change a system – or at the very least, empower teachers within that system – to teach students to write well, so there will always be good writers in this world, because in the words of Robert Frost: "No tears in the writer, no tears in the reader." I do not think Frost was referring to the many tears my students – or I - have cried as they sat for a timed, standardized writing assessment on a ridiculous prompt. Someone, some teacher, empowered the writers of those books we love. We must provide that access now, for the one sitting in our classroom, before it is too late. I began to apply these concepts I encountered through the readings I was exposed to in that graduate course to my own classes, with what I already knew was effective. And I simultaneously began a quest to uncover more research on writing instruction, and also read what writers themselves had to say, and really determine relevant, authentic, and best practices for today's writing classroom – those that would marry accountability with meaning.

In the months that followed I would effectively teach more students of varied abilities, and teach them all types of writing for multiple purposes, with great results. I experimented with my advanced and special education students alike, in small workshop groups, large classroom settings, and one on one. The research about writing instruction cannot be ignored, especially now when such emphasis is put on standardized assessment tests. "We end up helping students to write formulaically and superficially and to approach writing as pure performance rather than meaning making" (Agnew and McLaughlin 94). Had I fallen victim to this, I wondered? Had I taught my students to write "well enough" to pass the tests, but not really to move anyone or make a difference – and in doing so, had I "sold out?" There is a polarizing pendulum, that those of us who have been in the business awhile have seen swing too far out in one direction or another in many areas of English instruction: emphasize grammar and correctness – then don't be too critical and just encourage the writing process;

emphasize creative and personal writing - then, academic and argument writing; read for pleasure - read the classics; portfolio assessment versus one timed writing response. The pendulum had shifted once again with "No Child Left Behind" but this time, had I inadvertently and gradually gone with it? I had kept my bar higher than those standards measured on assessment tests, knowing they represented the minimum, and yet, on many levels, they had still come to dictate my own instruction, even, in some cases, by design. Aarrgh! Shouldn't expert research in the field of writing – and good writing itself - dictate that instruction and not a test?

Amazingly, I learned that through the years and pendulum shifts, much of the research about writing instruction has been consistent; it is the politics – and politicians – that have changed. Today one change has occurred that is not going away: transparency. For some of the public, and certainly the powers that sign our checks, this transparency is achieved largely by accountability ratings, derived from state or national assessment tests. What are we doing in our classrooms to teach good writing, the public wants to know, writing that colleges and corporations demand? And we echo, what are we doing to teach good writing, writing that someone loves to read, writing that can empower students, and make a difference in the way they understand and contribute to the world around them? Can we teach writing in such a way that accomplishes multiple goals? Can we do anything – even one thing – better, if armed with viable research and theories about what works for different learners? I decided I must care enough to find out. And what I found is that not only can we do better to prepare our students for the test, and teach meaningful writing – we can do both simultaneously.

Adrienne Rich remarked in her article, "Teaching Language in Open Admissions" more than thirty years ago, that for her, "language has implied freedom" (24). As a reader and writer, someone with ability to express myself fluently, easily, even poetically or passionately, it is easy to take this freedom for granted. Teachers who have watched a student struggle to translate his or her thought, to express it verbally, to write it effectively, know that this freedom is not easily accessible by all. What is needed in the writing classroom are "approaches to helping students widen the scope of their linguistic resources while engaging their cognitive powers in the process of responding to the world and experience, and making meaning from it linguistically, for it is this process that makes possible the realization of that freedom" (Bernstein *Teaching Developmental Reading* 2). These approaches to writing instruction exist, that provide freedom for students, access to articulation and communication, entrance to and success in academic and technical careers and communities. There are specific areas in which research about writing instruction can influence and improve instruction on the ground, and consequently, enhance the overall quality of writing our young people produce. These include: the connection between what we read and how we think and talk about that reading, and what we subsequently ask students to write; the knowledge that writing is a social act, and that communication with peers should be encouraged throughout the writing process, and a purpose and audience provided that is meaningful to the students; grammar instruction that is part of the overall context and purpose of literacy and communication; techniques specific for teaching "basic" writers or English language learners, at grade level and in preparation for the same assessments; and assessment practices that go beyond the test to drive curriculum and pedagogy.

After years of what most would label a successful career in the classroom, I began to formulate my own philosophy of writing instruction, grounded not just in my own instincts as a writer, or even my own classroom experiences, though certainly both are part of it, but in the research and findings of dozens of my colleagues and experts in the field, and in the performance and conversations of my own students. Though the research may confirm much of what I, and many English teachers, already know about writing and writing instruction, it is good to revisit it, to be validated, sometimes shocked, at the least encouraged, and often, inspired. My initial reluctance to attend that graduate class in basic writing theory grew into renewed enthusiasm to teach, as I witnessed the enhanced, authentic learning that occurred in my students as a result of my practical applications of the current theory and research about writing instruction.

The Reading-Writing Connection

"Reading a book can make you want to write one."
-Francine Prose

FRANCINE PROSE, AUTHOR OF MULTIPLE FICTION, NON-FICTION, young adult and children's books, credits reading with teaching her how to write: "A good teacher can show you how to edit your work. The right class can form the basis of a community that will help and sustain you…[But] I learned to write by writing, and by example, by reading books." (*Reading Like a Writer* 2) Stephen King concurs: "If you want to be a writer, you must do two things above all others: read a lot and write a lot" (139). In fact, research, such as that reported by Sugie Goen-Salter, Karen Uehling, Marcia Dickson, and Beth Hartman and Elaine Tarone, clearly supports a connection between reading and writing. Acknowledging this connection and implementing good texts into writing instruction is a first step in improving student writing in every stage of the process. This is not a new concept; rather, one that writers have always known: "Read, read, read. Read everything – trash, classics, good and bad, and see how they do it. Just like a carpenter who works as an apprentice and studies the most. Read! You'll absorb it. Then write" (William Faulkner). Teaching meaningful, effective writing requires us to move beyond summary, response, or five paragraph literary analysis and emphasize such things as student voice, perspective, experience, purpose, and choice – the very things books and essays model for students. Good writing can lead to ideas for students' own writing, provide a positive model for grammar and rhetorical instruction, and become a source of reference for students' own essays. Reading should spark student response to enter the conversation, but also model for students *how best to do that.*

The easiest way to tap motivation, first to read and then to write, is to teach students to choose books and other texts they understand and enjoy, and then to give them time in school to read them ("NCTE Beliefs About the Teaching of Writing"). Today, many students have family responsibilities or part time jobs. Many more have become addicted to "gaming" or "Facebook" and engage in these activities after school sometimes until four or five in the morning. Out of school reading may not be possible; it certainly is not probable. We have all wasted hours testing students on books they have not read and having discussions about literature with ourselves. It is imperative that in the midst of all the note-taking, writing, vocabulary drill, standardized test preparation, and group work, class time is allotted just for reading. I now understand that this is not just so they can process information, identify the theme or symbolism in the text, or engage in ethics discussions about the content, but most importantly, it is so they can learn to recognize and imitate, value and develop, *style*. And they will learn to write *correctly*. I realize I never had to be taught grammar in my life. I read early, often, and voraciously, and still do. Our students don't. No one read to many of them as children. They don't know what writing looks and sounds like. Our first task is to provide this access, the tools and exposure, through reading, if we ever expect them to be able – much less to desire – to write. "If [they] don't have time to read, [they] don't have the time (or the tools) to write" (King 142). Making students stronger readers, allowing time for reading in the classroom, also makes them stronger writers ("NCTE Beliefs About the Teaching of Writing"). This reading is not easy for all students; they are not used to reading academic texts, longer fiction, and non-fiction. They will be initally uncomfortable talking about writer's style and rhetorical choices. Teach the idea of a first, second, and third draft reading just as you teach drafting with writing. Not only does this facilitate interpretation of text, it enables students to identify, appreciate, and imitate writer style, and consequently, begin to understand the conventions that make up that style. Students may be encouraged or required to keep a log for each draft of reading: initial read and response; read for meaning, theme, symbols, literary elements; and read for style – diction, sentence structure, rhetoric, voice. This careful, multiple reading becomes a model that they may then apply to their own writing.

Teachers should select reading materials carefully. Most literature that does not engage students should be omitted from the curriculum, or teachers should find a way to make it relevant. We have students who don't want to read, struggle with reading, and seldom read anything for pleasure. If simply reading the material is a huge chore, it is likely understanding, discussing, and analyzing it will be out of the question. Teachers should question every single reading assignment they make, regarding potential to authentically engage students. Books that are enjoyable for students to read can be used to teach writing. In *Reading Like a Writer: A Guide for People Who Love Books and For Those Who Want to Write Them*, Francine Prose offers several excerpts of texts intended to help students benefit their writing. Citing such passages as the opening paragraphs of Flannery O'Conner's "A Good Man is Hard to Find" (16-19) and Katherine Mansfield's "The Daughters of the Late Colonel" (19-22), Prose demonstrates how a writer's choice of words and punctuation reveal more than a casual reader might think. This close reading is something students have to practice. It is not a natural way to read, especially for those used to rushing through to the conclusion or simply reading for basic information. They will have to be taught to think of reading in terms of author choices, and style: not just what happened, but *how* readers know what happened, and how we arrive at a certain understanding and feeling about the characters, the situation, the conflict, all dictated by the writer's choices. Students can be taught to use reading material as a model for their own writing, giving them this same power – *author*ity – over readers. What happens in the story becomes only one reason to read. Students will begin to understand that the author's style is what breathes the life into the story.

In my own 12th grade classroom and with my college freshmen I use Hemingway's "A Clean, Well-Lighted Place" and William Faulkner's "Barn Burning" for an assignment in tone and style. Students read both of the stories and respond to them, identifying characterization, theme, tone, all what one might expect from a literature class. They then re-read the stories, this time noting and comparing the specifics of each author's style. They are always enraged by Faulkner's bombastic vocabulary, as was Hemingway, who said, "Poor Faulkner. Does he really think big emotions come from big words?" (Quoted in A. E. Hutchner, Papa Hemingway). Students enjoy Hemingway's way of conveying emotion by showing instead of telling through his short, crisp, abrupt dialogue and simple sentences. On the other hand, his failure to identify who is speaking in the dialogue irritates many students, and they have to "count backwards" as one student said, to see who is talking, as in this example from "A Clean, Well-Lighted Place":

'He's drunk now,' he said.
'He's drunk every night.'
'What did he want to kill himself for?'
'How should I know?'
'How did he do it?'
'He hung himself with a rope.'
'Who cut him down?'
'His niece.'
'Why did they do it?'
'Fear for his soul.'
'How much money has he got?'
'He's got plenty.'
'He must be eighty years old.'
'Anyway I should say he was eighty.' (120-121)

From the sparse dialogue students infer more than they realized initially. They understand how less can be more, how the barrenness of the writing purposefully mirrors the theme.

Students are enamored, though, with Faulkner's remarkably detailed description and precise word choice, even while bemoaning his lengthy sentences, such as the following from "Barn Burning":

> Now he could hear his father's stiff foot as it came down on the boards with clocklike finality, a sound out of all proportion to the displacement of the body it bore and which was not dwarfed either by the white door before it, as though it had attained to a sort of vicious and ravening minimum not to be dwarfed by anything — the flat, wide, black hat, the formal coat of broadcloth which had once been black but which had now that friction-glazed greenish cast of the bodies of old house flies, the lifted sleeve which was too large, the lifted hand like a curled claw (129).

Students can talk about every part of that sentence. And that makes reading, about writing. They particularly enjoy the significance of "clocklike finality" (and yes, I may have to draw their attention to it initially), so perfect because in that step, in that moment, his father striding purposefully up the steps to the beautiful home with the white carpet, with horse manure all over his shoe, the boy, Sarty, saw all spoiled, again. The one descriptive sentence is longer than the whole of Hemingway's conversation, and thus reflects what Sarty thinks and feels about his father's long, oppressive presence that both he – and the reader – must endure. A study of the writing in this way enables students to discover how the tone of each of these selections is created by the author's choices. I have them locate and select another story by each of these authors and read it, summarizing and looking for consistency or disparity in style. I give them this writing exercise: write a dinner, vacation, or sports scene with their family or friends in their own style and voice; then write the same scene in the style of Hemingway; and again imitating Faulkner. Finally, they write about the entire experience and what they learned about writer choices, tone and style. Students who initially were adamant about preferring Hemingway, and getting lost in Faulkner, are surprised often to find that they write more like Faulkner; they also are surprised to find how hard it is to imitate Hemingway's style, which they believed would be the easier assignment of the two. Teachers can adapt this assignment for any grade level, choosing easier reading selections or those in their state curriculum or textbooks. The point is to choose literature that lends itself to a study of the language, and a study of writing styles that are effective in different ways. We want to make the reading about the writing, not about the short answer questions on content at the end of the story. This exercise gives students a purpose for reading, and connects reading to writing. It also enables them to understand the importance of style, or choices they make when they write. Of course, it is important to discuss everything – about the stories, the style, our own writing – but that is fodder for chapter three.

Karen Uehling suggests that reading full-length, challenging books, "especially books where language is focal," can help students become aware of how language is used. *The Poisonwood Bible* by Barbara Kingsolver and Leif Enger's *Peace Like a River* are current novels that provide excellent representations of authors' styles and language choices. In the former, Kingsolver utilizes the mother and each of four daughters in different chapters, each with different and unique voice, perspective and experience, to narrate their evangelical missionary dad's determined and doomed trip to Africa. Students recognize their own mothers, sisters, and themselves: in the mother's sacrifice; the oldest daughter's vain attempts to fix her hair and wear nice clothes, and in her suffering from lack of normal American teen-age activities; in one twin's hero-worship of the father; in the other twin's self-loathing; in the five- year- old's naïve enthusiasm and skewed reporting of the happenings in the jungle. They learn how the author uses persona to give perspective, and how our own perspective likewise affects and reflects our own stories and our own writing. In one chapter of this novel, we may study word choice; in another, imagery; in another, structure; and in several, characterization; and through it all, the author's choices, until the book is read and we know what happened, and *why* we responded the way we did to each voice and to the work as a whole. Stephen King said "Good writing, on the other hand, teaches the learning writer about style, graceful narration, plot development, the creation of believable characters, and truth-telling . . . You cannot hope to sweep someone else away by the force of your writing until it has been done to you" (141). My students love *The Poisonwood Bible* and thus, it truly inspires them to want to write better.

There are some books teachers believe must be taught because of school or state curriculum demands. But often there is room in the fine print for choice. There is no point to adhering to the same canon, however fabulous or necessary we believe it to be, if students aren't reading it, much less benefiting from it. Teachers will want to use novels appropriate for the students they teach – grade level, ability, interest – but often, the books we read for pleasure, our students will also enjoy and may serve us well in the classroom. One such book I implemented into my own curriculum was Enger's novel, *Peace Like a River*. The story is revealed rather like *The Adventures of Huckleberry Finn*: a young boy narrates a quest to find and save his outlaw older brother, while his own coming of age is expressed by Enger through colloquialisms, description, characterization, dialogue. It is unique in style as well: his young sister aspires to be a writer and her epic poem in progress is reported throughout the text. Uehling is right: students don't learn to read and love reading by our giving them simplified and unchallenging texts. They need to read something beautiful and amazing, and especially for the 11th and 12th grade students, they should read books that they will read as adults, so that they will learn to enjoy reading, and also figure out how to write. At the same time, we must choose carefully; it does no good to have these wonderful practical implementations of research on connecting reading and writing in our lesson plans if the students just will not read the material. It's not about the difficulty or the length; it's about the quality, and the connections that can be made through the literature.

Current non-fiction books and articles are very useful in this approach to connecting reading and writing as well. In addition to having access to a good non-fiction selection in the classroom and school library, students can peruse the Internet for best sellers and particular areas of interest. Among the non-fiction selected by my students for recent reading/writing projects: *A Long Way Gone* by Ishmael Beah (which our department now uses as a class set with 9th graders); *Eat, Pray, Love* by Elizabeth Gilbert; *Blue Like Jazz* by Dennis Miller; *Where Men Win Glory*, by Jon Krakauer; various motivational or self-help books by entrepreneurs, politicians, and successful athletic coaches; and Pat Conroy's autobiographical beauty, *My Losing Season*. Students enjoy analyzing style as well as content of books like these: first, what's the story; and second, how is the story presented – specifically, what narrative devices, story-telling tools, rhetorical choices - including vocabulary, voice, sentence structure, mode, diction, organization, and more - does the author use to make the writing effective? They present to the class not only the themes in their choice book, but also excerpts that illustrate writer choices and style. Their eventual assignment is to write their own ideas or stories in the style of the non-fiction they read, an assignment which in itself is research based: "students learn to write by discovering the validity and variety of their own experience"(Rich 19). To assign students to write this type of non-fiction without their ever having read some would cause confusion, fear, frustration, and ultimately, poor quality. This exposure enables them to see how a variety of authors tell their stories, and to realize that they likewise have a story to tell. They imitate the style that works in the non-fiction reading while drafting their own chapters, a written culmination of motivation, opportunity, and means.

The research is overwhelming: success in reading facilitates success in writing, and vice versa. Teachers must use this knowledge to advantage in our classrooms by connecting the two. Susan Bernstein reinforces this integration of reading into the basic writing classroom by citing a strong link between students' scores on the reading and writing skills tests ("The Impact of State Mandated Testing on Basic Writing" par 7). Goen-Salter agrees: "Better writers do tend to read more than poorer writers and better readers tend to produce more mature prose… When reading and writing are taught as separate subjects, these [benefits] are lost." This is logical, as both of these are really skills of articulation and communication: one (reading), with what comes in; and the other (writing), with what goes out. We articulate text and make meaning in our minds while we read; or we articulate thought and make meaning in text when we write. The need then is to provide integrated critical practice with writing and reading rather than teaching them as separate units with separate skills and drills. What we choose for students to read in our English classrooms must be purposeful and connected to writing.

But, learning to write through reading is not just about writing summaries or having original ideas for response to literature. "The present vogue for teaching 'values' through literature uses the novel as a springboard for the sort of discussion formerly conducted in civics or ethics classes . . . and everything about it that is inventive, imaginative, or pleasurable – is beside the point in classrooms, as is everything that constitutes style and that distinguishes writers" (Prose "I Know Why the Caged Bird Cannot Read" (93). We that are readers understand the pleasure Prose speaks of; we have read a book slowly, savoring each word because it is beautiful, graceful, like a dance or an opera. A good mystery novel may be rushed through to conclusion, but there are writers whose words and sentences must be bitten off and chewed, swirled and savored; these have the lingering finish of a fine wine – and that has nothing to do with plot outline or main idea and everything to do with language. Thematic subjects give the students something to connect with, and that is important as a place to begin discussions of literature. They may identify with the bad parenting of Willy Loman in Arthur Miller's *Death of a Salesman* or the abusive father in Sue Monk Kidd's *Secret Life of Bees*. Madness, greed, young love, sibling rivalry, and betrayal all may draw them in to Shakespeare, and certainly they will want to talk about love and war while reading *A Farewell to Arms*. This type of discussion introduces text, opens doors, and allows connections. But if we are teaching writing as well as reading, we must not study the Dust Bowl in *The Grapes of Wrath* and miss Steinbeck's storytelling skills:

> And here's a story you can hardly believe, but it's true, and it's funny and it's beautiful. There was a family of twelve and they were forced off the land. They had no car. They built a trailer out of junk and loaded it with their possessions. They pulled it to the side of 66 and waited. And pretty soon a sedan picked them up. Five of them rode in the sedan and seven on the trailer, and a dog on the trailer. They got to California in two jumps. The man who pulled them fed them. And that's true. But how can such courage be, and such faith in their own species? Very few things would teach such faith. The people in flight from the terror behind – strange things happen to them, some bitterly cruel and some so beautiful that the faith is refired forever (122).

A successful writing classroom must examine *why, and how,* the language of this passage moves us to contemplate human nature, rather than just to do so.

My 12th grade students recently read *Pride and Prejudice* by Jane Austen. Oh, the groaning, the complaining, the failure to see anything relevant or current in her writing, much less delightful, as I had so boldly advertised; and in fact, I was forced to confront my own standard for reading assignments – their potential for authentic student engagement. Before throwing up my hands altogether in despair and resignation, I began to point out her rhetorical and stylistic choices, through specific activities such as this one: I had students find a passage and imitate Austen's delightful (my students still shudder when I use the word), instructive, and exemplary style: the use of colons, semi-colons, sentence structure, formal diction, wit, understatement, and irony. What fun we had! This allowed students to connect the content to their own lives, and gave them a purpose for reading: to imitate the writing style in their own writing. Imitating a successful author encourages students to expand their knowledge base and forces them out of their comfort zone. For example, a student who does not know how to use semi-colons correctly has to learn for this assignment, and learns not on worksheets of skill and drill but through writing. Students began to recognize the nuances of sarcasm and satire and how their word choice makes that distinction. A particular favorite was the following passage, which several students imitated to write about classmates who were dating:

> Mr. Darcy had at first scarcely allowed her to be pretty: he had looked at her without admiration at the ball; and when they next met, he looked at her only to criticize. But no sooner had he made it clear to himself and his friends that she had hardly a good feature in her face, than he began to find it was rendered uncommonly intelligent by the beautiful expression of her dark eyes. To this discovery succeeded some others equally mortifying. Though he had detected with a critical eye more than one failure of perfect symmetry in her form, he was forced to acknowledge her figure to be light and pleasing; and in spite of his asserting that her

manners were not those of the fashionable world, he was caught by her easy playfulness (21)

One student creatively substituted her feelings about the church as the theme of her passage, which is reprinted here just as she wrote it:

At first I had not agreed with the 'church'; I looked at the 'church' in disgust; and the next time I went, I only sat there and criticized. But no sooner had I made it clear to myself and my friends that the 'church' had hardly a good aspect, then I began to find it was rendered uncommonly intelligent by the warm feeling of its fellowship. To this discovery succeeded some others equally mortifying. Though I had detected with critical thought more than one failure in its seemingly perfect leaders, I was forced to acknowledge the youth to be sweet and inspiring; and in spite of my initial asserting that some requirements were not that of most churches, I was blinded by the fact that it seemed normal now. Of all this, the 'church' was perfectly unaware; to the church I was just an active youth member, who saw more wrong than right with the institution.

Another student chose the famous opening passage:

It is a truth universally acknowledged, that a single man in possession of a good fortune, must be in want of a wife. However little known the feelings or views of such a man may be on his first entering a neighborhood, this truth is so well fixed in the minds of the surrounding families, that he is considered the rightful property of some one or other of their daughters (Austen 1).

And her parody:

It is a truth universally acknowledged, that a salutatorian in possession of a good brain, must be in want of a degree in a hard science or math. However little known the strengths or interests of such a student may be on her first entering a college, this truth is so well fixed in the minds of the surrounding teachers and family members, that she is considered the rightful property of some school or other of engineering or other math.

But students will not acknowledge the benefits of studying the language of literary texts, and connect these passages to their own writing, unless we make them slow down, unless we emphasize author style and choices, instead of just asking them who, what, when and where questions about content on a reading quiz (or a state assessment!). And yet, they will certainly be successful on the latter if they have gained the added benefits of instruction in purposeful, connected reading and writing.

We as readers would not want to rush to the conclusion of Shakespeare's tragedies and miss the artistry that propels us:

'Dark night strangles the traveling lamp' (*Macbeth*);

'What a piece of work is a man! how noble in reason!
how infinite in faculty! in form and moving how
express and admirable! in action how like an angel!
in apprehension how like a god! the beauty of the
world! the paragon of animals! And yet, to me, what
is this quintessence of dust? Man delights not me'
(*Hamlet*);

'O, I have bought the mansion of a love, But not
possess'd it, and, though I am sold, Not yet enjoy'd'
(*Romeo and Juliet*);

and from *King Lear*, a favorite of mine:

'No, no, no, no! Come, let's away to prison:
We two alone will sing like birds i' the cage:
When thou dost ask me blessing, I'll kneel down,
And ask of thee forgiveness: so we'll live,
And pray, and sing, and tell old tales, and laugh
At gilded butterflies, and hear poor rogues
Talk of court news; and we'll talk with them too,
Who loses and who wins; who's in, who's out;
And take upon's the mystery of things,
As if we were God's spies: and we'll wear out,
In a wall'd prison, packs and sects of great ones,
That ebb and flow by the moon.'

To read language such as this solely for information, to identify
theme, to have historical, philosophical, or ethical discussions -
would be a tragedy. The key for teachers is to begin to notice the
language and rhetoric more in the literature we already teach.

Wade into a discussion about language without fear. If we as teachers learn along with our students, that is even better. I had many "Aha!" moments as I began to apply the research and ideas I uncovered to my own curriculum and instruction. When discussions of literature can be steered to style and rhetorical choice, the written word, each word, the beauty of the language itself becomes an end and not a means to an end. A great benefit to reading this way becomes that students are also taught through the literature how to write – in what voice, in what form, for what purpose and audience, and in what style.

Making connections to good literature may provide motivation and lead to an authentic writing lesson. But it is not enough that students bring to the discussion their own history and experience, knowledge of author's life or understanding of plot, even appreciation of different styles and rhetoric. This may give them something to write about, but not teach them how best to write it, when they are seeking not imitation but their own voice and style and form. They are often at a loss when they have to make these choices themselves in writing assignments. Motivation without means or method is just frustrating. Access to that elusive writing code must include a study of writing itself: word- by- word, paragraph- by- paragraph, page by page. This is the hard part, the "how" of instruction. It is much easier to read something entertaining, answer a few comprehension questions, and move on. "Colonel Sanders sold a hell of a lot of fried chicken, but I'm not sure anyone wants to know how he made it" (King 80). But the place students can begin to appreciate and acknowledge language in literary text is in the kitchen, so to speak. We must teach them "how he made it" if we want them to make it for themselves. Francine Prose agrees: "To experience the heartbreaking matter-of-factness with which Anne Frank described her situation seems more useful than packing a paper bag with Game Boys, cigarettes, and CDs so that we can go into hiding and avoid being sent to the camps" ("I Know Why the Caged Bird Cannot Read" 98). Activities like these that focus on the "what" but not the "how" – the *effect* of the story on readers but not *how or why* that effect was achieved - may entertain or move readers to understanding, but do not empower them to write. "While linguistics and the science of language have developed, instructors in rhetoric and composition have become disconnected from its principles, and basic concepts that could shine clear light on the way instead remain unknown or ignored, disregarded" (Bernstein *Teaching Developmental Reading* 24). This kind of light-shining - access – to language must be provided by the teacher.

As classroom teachers, we ask students to write personal narratives, compare/contrast, causal analysis, documented literary analysis, and argumentative essays. But typically, we *read* fiction: short stories, plays, novels, poetry. "High schools seldom have students read non-fiction texts. In a recent look at several senior English books the only non-fiction offering was 'A Modest Proposal' by Johnathan Swift, hardly a non-fiction text to engage readers who don't usually read for pleasure." (Dickson). How are students to write quality non-fiction if they haven't read any? It is not difficult to incorporate student and professional examples of quality non-fiction in various genres into thematic literature. Teach the personal narrative with any coming of age short story, novel or epic hero journey; but also read professional and student non-fiction narrative essays. Print them out or put them on an overhead so students can see them. They need to view multiple finished products, and discuss how writer's purpose, intended audience, voice and content dictate style, form, and appeal. Students will begin to understand how to determine their own voices and stories when they are given the tools – exposure – to do so. It is unfair to ask them to make writing choices blindly.

I like to have students write a personal narrative before I teach it, then allow them to develop it and revise it multiple times as we examine various narratives of writers at all levels with various backgrounds and styles. This is a great way to assess instruction and see firsthand the difference access can make in writing. Maya Angelou's "Champion of the World", a chapter from her autobiography I Know Why the Caged Bird Sings, works well for teaching elements of narration and description; students can easily locate examples of her vivid dialogue, figurative language, tropes, and colloquialism. Students will talk about why her narrative reads more like a story than theirs and is more entertaining to the reader. Francine Prose criticizes the use of Angelou in the classroom; she calls her prose "murky, turgid, convoluted" with simple meaning obscured in multiple metaphors ("I Know Why the Caged Bird Cannot Read" 92). And maybe it is a little over the top. But for my purposes in the high school classroom, Angelou has served us well, particularly to demonstrate the idea of "showing" instead of "telling" in personal writing. When teaching students to use figurative language in description, to consider perspective, and to connect seemingly small experiences to larger life lessons, I share with them Annie Dillard's "The Snake," or "Living Like Weasels". They can easily identify all elements of description and imitate her style in their own writing. "How I Lost the Junior Miss Pageant" by Cindy Bosley is a narrative essay that provides students a study in voice, poignant reflection, aesthetic distance, and organization. Through reading these essays, students can learn to recognize anecdotes, figurative language, power words and phrases, and stylistic, syntactical and rhetorical devices in professional essays; and also, to imitate these in their own writing. They gain access to the realm of possibility for their own finished product, and the confidence they need to tell their own stories. This is the application that is so often lost, even in our advanced classes where students are taught to analyze rhetoric. They can't truly appreciate writing until they have incorporated what they know works - from their reading - into their own writing. After reading a few professional, and some past student, narratives during the instruction process, my own students' writing developed tremendously. This access made all the difference.

It is not just with personal narratives or description that I use professional examples. I teach them how they might set up compare/contrast essays and then let them see how others blend and vary the methods and modes for interest and effectiveness and audience. We read sample essays such as Deborah Tannen's "Sex, Lies and Conversation: Why Is It So Hard for Men and Women to Talk to Each Other?" (*The Washington Post*, June 24, 1990) and talk about why it works. My students learn that mature, interesting essays often compare inner growth instead of surface factors; they learn to compare the *why's* as well as the *what's*. We review and write comparisons of literature, scientific theories, religions, philosophies or personalities. With causal analysis I introduce Joan Didion's "In Bed", an essay in which she explores the causes and effects of migraines, and personalizes the essay by including her own coping mechanism, allowing readers to enter the conversation on many levels. Students discuss all the possible connections they bring to the essay, substitute their own topics, and then experiment with their own styles. This method of exposing students to a variety of professional essays is especially effective with academic argument writing, as rhetorical theorists have asserted that much of writing is responding to what others have said (Graff and Birkenstein ix). With argument, I like to use Ward Churchill's "Crimes Against Humanity" or John Wallace's "The Case Against Huck Finn" because students are familiar with that content. We also read some of the essays from Jay Allison and Dan Gediman's *This I Believe: The Personal Philosophies of Remarkable Men and Women* to spur interest in and discussion of students' own beliefs. Through access such as this students learn to examine, formulate, and articulate for others their own beliefs and philosophies. They learn what they think first, and then, how to express it. It is invaluable for them to *see* how sources are used: how they are introduced, paraphrased, quoted, and cited. Sure, we can teach this, but how much easier on the students – and us - it would be if they were not starting from scratch – if they were used to accessing and reading works in this style already, available in scholastic journals, online and in online data bases such as EBSCO. Documented argument papers would not be foreign or fearsome, but rather, an opportunity for students to contribute to the conversations around them in a correct and credible manner. Through various styles of argument and documentation, students will begin to recognize when invective tone turns them off, when emotional pleas are effective, when use of parallelism or repetition emphasizes a point and builds to a climax, when sources are credible or laughable. If they do not read academic argument, assigning them to write one is like asking me to design a web page or speak Chinese tonight at dinner. It isn't practical, and sets them up to fear and to fail.

Viewing professional essays in a variety of modes provides access and awareness to students faced with what at first may to them appear to be daunting and unfamiliar assignments. There are many good examples of essays like those mentioned above, available in any college writing text, in magazines or journals, online, and in the world around us, for all of the writing tasks we give our students. Students can even find them. I use different ones from year to year depending on the make-up of the class, their ability level, interests, and experiences. In my class, we often read student essays I have kept over the years that are particularly effective for one reason or another, and I love showing these because students see that although they may not be "perfect" grammatically the writing has merit and is entertaining. Initially, and especially with the professional essays, this practice of juxtaposing student work with models may cause them to "see [their] own work in a most unflattering light"(Prose *Reading Like a Writer* 9), or "fill a new writer with feelings of despair and good old-fashioned jealousy" (King 141). But students need something to which to aspire; they need direction provided by viewing these finished products. This practice focuses some the discussion of the classroom literature and reading on language and rhetoric, as opposed to just providing a forum for summative response and philosophical discussions.

Prose insists that "It's become a rarity for a teacher to suggest that a book might be a work of art composed of words and sentences, or that the choice of these words and sentences can inform and delight us" (Prose "I Know Why the Caged Bird Cannot Read"). This has been magnified by the reading- for -information style of many state assessments. As classroom writing teachers, it makes far more sense to read for pleasure, and to inspire and inform writing. Amy Tan said to Stephen King in a discussion about questions from fans, "No one ever asks about the language" (King xiv). Yet getting a great idea for a book or essay is but a small component of the writing process. As teachers of writing, we *have* to ask about the language, and teach about the language. Writing should not become a second or third language for our students, to be translated and struggled with in the classroom, but not used at home or at play. Indeed, although we don't label it, at times I think we have to teach WSL – Writing as a Second Language, or WLL – Writing Language Learners. This doesn't have to be the case. With enough exposure to a variety of good writing in all genres and styles and of all lengths and difficulties, our students' understanding of what writing is will be developed. They will become more confident and willing to write themselves, and their writing won't be a shot in the dark, but purposefully crafted, as they learn to use the stylistic and rhetorical choices they have recognized in reading. In his book *On Writing* King sets forth a brief passage and suggests "We could have a fifty minute writing class on just this brief passage," encompassing dialogue, phonetically rendered language, the use of the comma, even "the decision not to use the apostrophe. . ." (126-127). Classroom teachers can do this with a passage from any reading selection in our current curriculum. Students may discuss in small groups the writing, the construction of a paragraph, down to the smallest detail. This type of modeling provides access to a study of language – the professional writer's and the student writer's - and gives students options. As such, it is an important component of the reading-writing connection.

We are not born knowing how to write. Students, especially those who are not reading on their own, do not know how to join the conversation around them, unless they are exposed to a subject and methods of articulation. A great deal of that exposure can be provided by a good variety of classroom reading. In addition to good novels, full- length non-fiction, and professional essays that model various modes of composition and rhetoric, teachers can use poems throughout the year as well, that reflect these diverse essay modes and rhetorical choices, to show that the development and expression of ideas in writing is not limited to any genre. Like all reading selections these will vary from year to year, according to grade, maturity, interest and ability level of students, but following are some of the poems I have had success teaching as part of writing instruction. With compare/ contrast writing, Dorothy Parker's "General Review of the Sex Situation" (really good with the aforementioned Tannen essay on same subject); "Fire and Ice" by Robert Frost; or two poems, such as the original "Shall I Compare Thee to a Summer's Day" (Shakespeare 1564-1616) and the subsequent parody of the same name by Howard Moss (1923-1987). With causal analysis reading and writing, "White Lies," by Natasha Tretheway, and "My Husband Discovers Poetry" by Diane Lockward. I might use D.H. Lawrence's "Piano" or Robert Frost's "Out, Out" with our unit on narration and reflection; for tone, Ambrose Bierce's "The New Decalogue" (didactic, satiric); for figurative language, "The Eagle" by Alfred, Lord Tennyson and "Chicago" by Carl Sandburg. Language is not naturally expressed through compartmentalized writing: grammar, poetry, rhetoric, fiction, creative, or argument. It is all around us, available and accessible for every purpose, appropriate in some form for every audience.

Once students start understanding this, they began to think of their own stories in these broad terms, and their writing really takes off. The disconnect between reading and writing in our own classrooms must be addressed to allow students to connect writing tasks to their lives and the real world, and think of themselves as "real" writers.

One of the assumptions identified in the Position Statement about Writing Assessment released by the Conference on College Composition and Communication in 1995 is that students should write on "real-world" prompts developed from the curriculum. This is to make writing assignments that allow students to make connections between the literature they have read in the classroom and their own life stories. But writing instruction is more than this. "It's about the day job; it's about the language" (King xv). If students have been exposed to all the modes and different techniques of composition in the classroom, through the examples provided by the teacher, they will see in the literature so much more than opportunities for summary and analysis – real possibilities for their own writing, whether personal narrative, causal analysis or argumentative editorial. They will begin to articulate their own stories - with voice, complex sentence structure - unconsciously and consciously making choices they have seen in the literature and professional essays. With this kind of access to reading material comes more understanding of desired outcome on writing assignments, and less fear. Students feel empowered to make choices; they take ownership of the writing. "Reading . . . creates an ease and intimacy with the process of writing . . . It also offers [students] a constantly growing knowledge of what has been done and what hasn't, what is trite and what is fresh, what works and what just lies there dying (or dead) on the page" (King 145). And when students own the writing, they care more about the quality. Reading *The Grapes of Wrath* should give students pause. But in truth, teachers must *insist* they pause, and locate text that "sounds" beautiful, that is beautiful. In that novel, it's easy, and soon they are pointing out the language on their own. And after reading *The Grapes of Wrath*, students can make connections and choices and write about personal journeys, natural disasters, inner strength, immigration reform, prison, dying for a cause, prejudice, pregnancy, and much more, in diverse, articulate, stylistic – and yes, beautiful - ways. They will use compound sentences, colloquialisms, unique points of view, stream of consciousness, fragments, and dashes. Writing students must recognize not just that Faulkner and Hemingway are different, but why they are different, and the effects of the differences on readers. We want them to recognize manipulation of language and start taking risks in their writing. This goes so far beyond writing for a timed assessment, and yet prepares students for it, without making that preparation a total bore, or the end goal of writing instruction.

It is common sense that professionals learn to write for their vocation by reading articles written by others in the field. This logic certainly applies to the writing classroom. Teachers must be made aware of the research on the reading/writing connection, decide what constitutes "critical practice" and apply these techniques in their classrooms. In this way we facilitate the writing process as much as we instruct in it, by not making our anticipated outcome a secret, and by providing for students some prior knowledge – tools – on which to build. They will remember when confronted with writing tasks what outcome looks like, and know what readers – because they are now readers – want. King's allusion to fried chicken was right on. If we don't teach students to navigate the kitchen and produce the five-star meal, they'll be eating fast food all their lives.

CHAPTER TWO

Writing as a Social Act

"Who's Going to Read This, Anyway?"
-a student

IN ADDITION TO GIVING STUDENTS THE OPPORTUNITY, means, and methods to write successfully, we can provide greater motivation, if we as teachers get out of the way, and allow them to interact with and write for their peers. One reason teachers are frustrated is there seems to be no intrinsic motivation in our students to revise. They will attempt to edit, if only to get a higher grade, but real revision – examining and rethinking choices they make as writers - rarely occurs. They are content with whatever comes out of their minds and onto the paper first. Yet Ernest Hemingway said "Every first draft is s---," and Francine Prose notes, "All the elements of good writing depend on the writer's skill in choosing one word instead of another. And what grabs and keeps our interest has everything to do with those choices." (Prose *Reading Like a Writer* 16). One of the challenges of writing instruction is teaching students to make – and remake - these choices. A greater challenge is getting them to want to. If students don't consider audience, they have no reason to choose carefully, as they have nothing invested; there is no one they are trying to stir, to gain approval from, to affect. Current research shows that writing is a social act, and that when they have a meaningful audience, students view writing not as an isolated chore but as a social interaction process with peers.

Students need to discuss composition before, during, and after the writing process.

> As they grow, writers still need opportunities to talk about what they are writing about, to rehearse the language of their upcoming texts and run ideas by trusted colleagues before taking the risk of committing words to paper. After making a draft, it is often helpful for writers to discuss with peers what they have done, partly to get ideas from their peers, partly to see what they, the writers, say when they try to explain their thinking ("NCTE").

This is more than the read-analyze-write model traditionally applied to writing about literature (Hartman and Tarone 382). It certainly opposes the isolated, timed, "respond to a prompt" writing assessment. Students need to verbalize to each other what they want to say so they can find out themselves. I find this to be true even when I talk to students one on one:

Teacher: 'What topic are you considering?
Student: 'Racism.
Teacher: 'What about it?
Student: Silence. Then: 'Well, you know, it's bad.

Teacher: 'Do you mean towards a certain race?

Student: 'I don't know. Like, why people do it, I guess.

Teacher: 'You want to talk about what causes racism?

Student: 'Yeah, like some people grow up with parents who are racists, so they are.

Teacher: 'Do you have specific examples you are thinking of?

Student: 'That's what I'm saying. Dude, the other day, me and my friends were…

Teacher: 'That is really awful. You might want to start with that story to grab your reader's attention. What do you think?

Student: 'Yeah, but then how do I make it about the world and not just my race?

Teacher: 'Do you want to talk specifically about something that happened to you, or try to get people not to do it, or both?'

And so on. By leading the student into a discussion I can lead him to understand why he chose the topic, what in particular he wants to say about it, and what format and voice his paper should take - argumentative, personal narrative, causal analysis. As we talk his writing takes shape and he is able to form a clear thesis and organize his thoughts. It is imperative that students answer these questions before they begin writing or they have no direction. How much different – and better – the results on state assessments would be if students were allowed to verbalize what they are being asked, and verbalize a response, to even realize their own opinions and knowledge before they begin to try to articulate this on paper for a stranger. Yet when given a topic, most students just start writing. Many don't even pre-write; they plop a title on the top line and write straight through with no idea or method whatsoever, thinking that because it has always been good enough to pass – because they have adequate understanding of grammar and style and can write sentences without error - it must be good enough, period. Others, particularly the students with learning disabilities or those in the special education population, can't think of anything to write at all. They don't know how to even begin. Conversation about the writing benefits both of these groups. Teachers can instruct students to learn to discourse about writing among themselves. "Students best discover what they want to say not by thinking about a subject in an isolation booth, but by reading texts, listening closely to what other writers say, and looking for an opening in which they can enter the conversation. In other words, listening closely to others and summarizing what they have to say can help writers generate their own ideas." (Graff and Birkenstein xiii) They need to "enter a conversation, using what others say (or might say) as a launching pad or sounding board for [their] own ideas." (3) If we model and teach this conversing before, about and during the writing process in the classroom, it will become a practice, a habit, which our students will eventually initiate themselves in their own writing lives.

I use social interaction with my students when we first begin argument or persuasive writing, to enable them to see all sides of an issue, and to see how anticipating the other side's arguments can strengthen their own. We play a conversation game called "R U Nuts?" that I swiped somewhere, like most good ideas, and adapted to meet the needs of my own classroom. (The students changed the title to text-speak.) In the game, one group member states his thesis clearly for the others, who then have two minutes to write down everything they can think of that *opposes* his argument, even if they actually agree with his statement. At the end of two minutes, they take turns saying, "R U Nuts?" and reading aloud the list they have made. The "Nut" writes notes, to use as material to anticipate, refute, or compromise on in his own paper, thus strengthening it. When all students have shared, they discuss in which areas there may exist common ground, which are not strong enough to really be included, and on which points neither side is likely to give at all and what can be done about it. From peer reaction, student writers are able to learn where their own content is strong and where it is weak, what they should start with or omit altogether, etc. And, it's a fun way for them to enter the conversation about controversial topics, and to talk -with enthusiasm -about writing.

Students should interact at various stages during the process as well as prior to it, to ascertain that direction, purpose, and voice are clear. This is more than just peer revision and it certainly is more than peer editing. I am not a fan of the "switch papers and read" version of peer revision. Students tend to only edit and compliment each other's writing instead of really offering constructive help. It isn't that they don't want to help each other; they don't know how. Again, access is the key. Teachers need to provide a rubric initially that guides students through the revision process. For example, have a few group members listen while a writer reads her paper, and list three or four things that are strong in the writing and three or four things that are weak or unclear. The student who reads the paper then listens to the critique, taking notes and asking questions, but should be reminded not to argue. If she has to qualify or clarify something, this simply means her intent did not manifest in the paper, and how wonderful that she found out in this stage of the process when she can still improve the delivery. Groups can be as small or as large as needed.

Sometimes I do this activity with the entire class, remembering to have a different volunteer read his or her paper each time. At first, students were reluctant to volunteer; now, they want to because they see how much the feedback helps the writer. Interestingly, my students who are not good writers themselves – and all of the students in the class, in fact – are quick to offer feedback and constructive criticism to others. After hearing the paper read aloud and jotting down notes as they listen, students recently offered suggestions such as these:

'I didn't hear a thesis in your intro – did you have one?'

'Did you have any quotes? I think that would have made your paper stronger.'

'I think you got the names mixed up in paragraph two.'

'There was something in the third paragraph that didn't seem to fit with the rest. Can you read that to me again?'

'I like how easy it is to understand you, but you might want to use some bigger words. It's sort of simple.'

This really contributes to the confidence of the critics, who realize that they do have enough knowledge about writing to help someone else, and consequently, to make good choices in their own writing. Sometimes, on a different assignment or on a second reading of the same assignment, I'll just put students in twos or threes to discuss the writing. At this stage I might have student authors record their intended effect on one side of a paper, and then have readers record the actual effect on the other, for comparison. Throughout the process and with the final product, students need to know they have an audience other than the teacher to authenticate for them the content and stimulate intrinsic desire to improve quality of style.

There are many classroom activities that affirm the benefits of the social aspect of the writing process. In one writing activity, I present my students with writing topics and give them a few days to compose drafts. I ask them to talk about the writing process in small groups before and during the process, and give them some simple questions with which to initiate discussion, such as the following:

Before completing a draft:

*What topics did you initially consider? Why?

*Is there a personal connection or motivation for your choice of topic?

*What is one thing you want to be clear in this paper?

*What modes could you use for this topic?

And after completing a draft, reading parts of it and again discussing in small groups:

*Did your direction change as you went through the process?

*Where could you use dialogue?

*What difficulties did you experience?

*Whose writing (that we have read in class) do you feel like yours most compares to?

*What is the best part of your paper – to you? To your audience?

*How is the paper organized? Is this the best way for your purpose, topic, and mode?

Results of this classroom activity also supported the research. As they discussed the writing assignment and process, student comments quickly shifted from those about style and form ("I suck at spelling") to those about depth and direction of the essays. One student said he realized he "didn't say what he wanted to say at all." A bonus, as one student articulated, was that "we didn't even talk about grammar in our group!" Guided discussions like these enable students to see that writing – and revising - is not just about editing; while at the same time, editing is improved as students become aware of audience and desire to make meaning clear, effective, and impressive for their classmates. Marti Singer refers to this phenomenon when she says, "I discovered that when students are clear about their focus and the meaning they want to make in writing, the usage errors tend to dissipate and the whole of their writing is more effective" (104). Though they would not think so, most teachers tend to see revision "as more of a correction process than a learning one" (Hartman and Tarone 383). In "Goals and Philosophies," Amy Levin shows that student tutors are more inclined to talk about how to fix and avoid errors instead of just correcting them, and they talk more about the process and rhetorical choices than a teacher does. This may be because the students realize teachers "know" how to correct their papers, and just want them to rapidly "fix" (edit) their work; with peers, they have to be convinced, and thus are more inclined to figure it out together. I have observed this with my own student tutors. They generally tell the students they are helping *why* something should be done differently, instead of just changing it for them on the page. As a result, "cognitive development is promoted as writing skills are enhanced" (Levin 27). All told, my students loved talking about their writing with classmates and were able to make better rhetorical and stylistic choices after doing so.

Another place I saw this social interaction in the writing process was in my after school writer's workshop for my struggling and basic writers. Having just recently encountered research about the social nature of writing, the first day of the workshop I resisted the impulse to assign seats or spread the students out at the tables in my classroom, letting them instead come in and sit where they wanted. As a writer who likes to be completely alone to write, with my materials spread out all around me, in complete quiet, I am always surprised and puzzled that students do not do this. They bunch together, four or five at a table, even leaving two tables completely empty. They blurt things out and don't seem to be bothered by someone else's blurting, near as much as I am. It all supports what research indicates about teaching writing, particularly to ELL students: the instruction should "introduc[e] cooperative, collaborative writing activities which promote discussion;" and "encourag[e] contributions from all students, and promot[e] peer interaction to support learning" ("NCTE Position Paper on the Role of English Teachers in Educating English Language Learners"). Indeed, as my students began to respond to short answer questions about a reading selection (a large component on the state assessment, which is intended to measure reading comprehension as well as students' ability to compose and articulate a good answer using support from selections), they automatically conferred with each other:

'What is the question asking?
What quote are you using?
'Is the brother or the dad the one who is learning something new?'

'How much do I have to write to get a good score, do you think?'

'Will you read mine?'

'How do you spell 'definitely'?'

When the time came for students to write an essay in the writing workshop, they immediately began chatting about experiences they could use, and through conversation with peers, formulated strategies for writing that included organization, leads, and general style and direction.

'What's it mean, independent? I don't think I am ever independent.

'It means you do stuff by yourself. You take care of yourself.

'I do everything by myself.

'I can't think of how to start.

'Well aren't you from another country? You don't even live with your parents!

'Oh.

'I had to fly all by myself once to see my dad and was stranded in the airport for fourteen hours. That is independent.

'I quit soccer so I could get a job and pay for my own stuff.

'That's just stupid.

'Yeah, but it's independent.

'Well how do I start?

'You could start in the airport when you just found out you were stranded.

'Good idea.

'I am going to talk about myself in third person, the little boy whose mom got sick and then end up with him taking care of himself.

'Yeah, that's cool.'

Without this conversation, some students would not have been able to even get started. Others would have written a shallow, boring essay on independence with no real examples, purpose, or appeal to audience. In this setting, not only did they talk about how to begin, but also read parts of their papers to each other for feedback, edited for each other, made suggestions throughout, and through encouragement and support, validated each other's experiences. They were authentically engaged throughout the writing process because the interaction with peers created not only a safe environment with less fear, but made the assignment meaningful.

This arrangement of students and the conversation may not be in all teachers' comfort zones, and certainly we may have to redirect from time to time, but overall, the students were on task, talking about writing, and helping each other. This is a great thing. The students will seat themselves near those with whom they are comfortable, and friendships may be formed or strengthened in addition to writing skills. I even occasionally allow my students the final say on each other's short answer scores, and they are very close to giving the exact same scores I would have assigned, though perhaps a little harder on each other than I am on them. We teachers tend to assess such things as effort, making allowances, subconsciously at least, for the learning or language deficiencies, or extenuating circumstances, of the writers. Students, although verbally more compassionate, actually tend to be unbiased when assigning grades. I love that they also do not underestimate each other. The writing workshop evolved into something wonderful, primarily because I acknowledged the research and encouraged the social interaction that took place freely that first day. And while I understand that some assessment settings require students to respond to a prompt in isolation, this is not an assessment setting. This is a learning environment, a writing classroom, and when students are *in the learning process and not the assessing process*, teachers must employ the research-based strategies with proven effectiveness. When students have gained the confidence, access, and skills necessary, through activities such as these, to write well, test-taking may be introduced *as a genre* of writing, and not the end goal or governing body of all classroom writing instruction.

Having witnessed by now the effectiveness of classroom applications of research on both the reading-writing connection and the social nature of writing, I tied these two concepts together in my classroom in a couple of ways. I have already mentioned that my students read *The Grapes of Wrath* by John Steinbeck in an 11th grade English class, so I'll use that book again for an example. In groups, students discussed many thematic and historical aspects of the novel, including writing style, immigration, natural disasters, personal journeys, and prejudice, as well as elements of style: use of poetic language, extended metaphors, speech patterns of the migrants, diction, and the use of inter-chapters. Applying the idea that "prompts [should be] developed from the curriculum and grounded in 'real-world' practice' (CCCC: "Writing Assessment") I asked students to use our discussions as springboards for their essays, and allowed them freedom to develop their own topics, purpose, audience, and style. I told them they could take any mode, for any audience, and I modeled a few ideas I might use if it were my own paper. I write (model) with students a lot, sharing with them my own concerns and struggles and processes as a writer. Just as it helps students to see sample products and published literature, it also helps them to see those they perceive as "writers" engaged in the process. They talked in small groups prior to writing, which helped them settle on general topics and then a thesis, direction and mode; during the writing process, which is when they addressed stylistic choices and organization through revision of drafts; and after the completion of final drafts, when they received more specific revising and editing help. The results were amazing. Mark (all names are changed) made the leap from the struggles of the Joads, the migrant family in *The Grapes of Wrath*, to his own struggles with skin cancer in a powerful personal narrative. Jessica first experimented with the diction and speech patterns of her own immigrant family, before deciding instead to use her personal experiences with prejudice and intolerance in an editorial in support of immigration reform. Andrea wrote her life in inter-chapters, imitating Steinbeck's style by alternating between journalistic commentary about current events and her own personal relationship journey. In my 12th grade English class we had similar experiences. After reading *Macbeth*, small group conversations generated diverse, authentic writing topics such as Amber's true tale of madness in a local citizen and Wanda's narrative of personal motivation and justification. Sean wrote a causal analysis essay on the effects of dysfunctional families; and Liam wrote about alcoholism as a tragic flaw in a prominent student athlete on campus. We enjoyed reading Mike's entertaining comparison of *Macbeth* to a modern day politician; and Judy's compelling argument that the witches were manifestations of good dreams gone bad, equally available to us today. Because we had made the connection that writing about literature does not have to be analysis, though that certainly is an option, and we had read many types of non-fiction essays in class in previous weeks and months, students felt confident in choosing topics and modes of expression, with or without textual support. That confidence grew as they interacted with peers and received encouragement throughout the process. Students were intrigued that we could all read the same thing, discuss it, and have such different writing responses to the same reading. They enjoyed the entire assignment more than most writing assignments. And, as a result of sharing their work with peers (a meaningful audience) students became personally invested, which improved quality and correctness.

Classroom teachers should explore other types of writing as well. In a break from the traditional, students may write "found" poems (Dunning and Stafford). In this exercise, teachers may choose to have students review a play or novel they have just completed, or bring in magazines, junk mail, and newspapers to examine. Students "plagiarize" by picking out favorite lines or words and then arranging them in any order, font, shape, or style they want on the page. My students love being told they do not have to "write" anything; rather, they are going to "find" a poem. Suppose we have just finished *Macbeth*. I have my students go back through the play, finding words, phrases, lines or even couplets that they like. Since we have just completed a fairly thorough study, they generally know where the lines are; however, part of the fun is hearing the class chatter while looking for their favorite lines: "I think Lady Macbeth said that in Act 2;" or "Dude, it's on page 417 – I just wrote that one down, too!" I tell them to look for language they like, but also, language that they can arrange to suggest a common theme, and I give them freedom to choose their punctuation. Popular themes are blood, death, guilt, politics, and love. One of my 12th grade boys wrote the following poem called

"Use Protection." He was trying to be cute, but actually illustrated the process quite well:

At first and last, a hearty welcome
Let's briefly put on manly readiness
Filthy Hags!!!
You made it known to us
Not in the legions of horrid hell
Can come a devil more damned
For they *hath given me fire*
Upon my head, they placed a fruitless crown
Filthy hags!!!
I am afraid to think of what I've done
I could not
Wash this filthy witness
Clean from my hands
Filthy hags!!!
I can buy me twenty at any market
That I to your assistance do make love
Hath cowed the better part of man.

The found poem not only takes some of the fear out of poetry for both teachers and students, but also exposes students to free verse, literary elements, language, and theme, and allows them to manipulate language for purpose and audience. We talk about what drew the students to the lines they selected: colloquialism, connotation, figurative language, alliteration, or rhythm. These are all choices writers may consciously make, and thus, the "found poem" exercise fits very well into the writing classroom. It provides an excellent representation of the social aspect of writing, as students converse throughout the process; and employs the reading-writing connection. It fosters a greater appreciation and understanding of language – a particular benefit when reading Shakespeare – and demonstrates manipulation of that language to accomplish purpose and theme.

Language is social and social interaction during the writing process is beneficial. Through such classroom activities as these, students will learn to engage in these practices themselves in personal writing assignments they encounter throughout their lives. These instructional methods will not prevent students from being successful in rigid conditions like state assessments or college entrance tests; on the contrary, through social discourse they will learn to better revise and edit their own writing when they have to, because their knowledge, comfort level, and confidence in the process and in their own choices will have been established. My students are already grounded in basic essay writing technique: creative titles, catchy introductions with clear thesis statements, multi-paragraphing, dialogue, voice, sentence structure. They receive this type of instruction throughout elementary, middle school and high school in our English department, and review it early and often in my own classes. This grounding – access – gives them the tools to enjoy greater freedom to make choices, take risks, and grow as writers as they are exposed to more challenging academic texts, ideas, and assignments. Activities like these that provide connection to the text and to an audience encourage students to take ownership of their writing, and results in much higher quality of essay content and style. This proves the first assumption set forth by the CCCC: "Language is always learned and used most effectively in environments where it accomplishes something the user wants to accomplish for particular listeners or readers within that environment" (CCCC "Writing Assessment: A Position Statement"). When writing conditions in our classrooms only mirror those types of isolated test settings and not what real writers do, it is no wonder most students hate writing and are ill prepared to write for meaningful purposes and audiences. I can attribute much of the improvement in my own student writers to the explicit reading-writing connection, coupled with the application of social interaction during the writing process.

Although our social interaction did not specifically include "peer revision" in the way students had always perceived it, primarily editing spelling or punctuation, correctness mattered more to them because they took ownership of the papers and had an audience other than me. I would contend, then, that there is another meaning to be made when the reading, writing and reflecting processes are integrated: editing. And so it is that through careful reading selections and guided social interaction, the instruction of grammar becomes less painful and more meaningful; thus, more effective.

CHAPTER 3

The Grammar Connection

"To tell a group of adolescents who already know how to
speak and write that that is the purpose of grammar is
like telling someone that they need to read a history of
toilets through the ages in order to pee and poop."
- 12 year old Paloma, in Muriel Barbery's
The Elegance of the Hedgehog

THE GRAMMAR DEBATE RAGES ON, AND BASED on my research,
has for a hundred years with varying conclusions. "It seems that
in the past several decades, in mainstream English Language Arts
and English as a Second Language (ESL) classrooms alike, the
pendulum of language pedagogy has swung from one extreme to
another" (Hagemann). Teachers of English at all levels disagree
whether knowledge of conventional grammar contributes to
better writing, what this knowledge actually is, and how best
to impart it to students. Quite frankly, there is enough research
to make a supported case for the teacher-centered skill and drill
teaching of grammar, or its omission in the writing classroom

altogether, though in more recent years the trend has been toward the latter. Neuleib and Brosnahan acknowledge that some research suggests that "instruction in traditional grammar over a limited period of time . . . showed no positive effect on students' writing" (146), but go on to say that "This dismissal of grammar teaching is unfortunate..." (149). Perhaps they express the quandary of many teachers: the inability to connect traditional, linear grammar instruction to the writing itself, and show its worth and meaning to students in the context of literacy and communication. This frustration leads to less formal classroom instruction, which then is reflected in inadequate and deficient student control of these elements in their writing. What is unfortunate is that teachers who dismiss these components altogether, instead of finding alternate ways to facilitate the same knowledge, through authentic and more productive lessons, realize too late that they have inadvertently thrown the baby out with the bathwater. Other writing instructors have begun to associate correctness with intolerance, blurring the line between product and people, like Ira Shor, who went so far as to claim that "correct usage represents an effort to extend dominant authority" (33). Whatever the reason, dismissing grammar instruction as naught to do with writing is something writers themselves, Francine Prose among them, recognize is detrimental: "Among the questions that writers need to ask themselves in the process of revision – Is this the best word I can find? Is my meaning clear? Can a word or phrase be cut from this without sacrificing anything essential: - perhaps the most important question is: *Is this grammatical?*" (*Reading Like a Writer* 43 my italics)

Uehling instructs teachers that "writing includes three major components: invention, arrangement and style. Grammar and correctness are just one part of style; further, invention and arrangement are usually considered more important than style". That depends on what stage of the writing process students are in, and what their goals, purpose, and audience are. All parts of writing contribute to the meaning and quality of product and to the response of the reader. A lack of correctness limits writers, not just in being able to say what they want to say, but in their effectiveness, academically and socially. "In our efforts to promote more content-centered pedagogy, we had to paint grammar in the most negative light possible, and in doing so, we lost sight of what was valuable about studying it. We forgot how much grammar and other forms *contribute to meaning*" (Hagemann, my italics). Hagemann has a point: as more and more content and resources are available, even required, teachers may feel compelled to let the least enjoyable elements of the curriculum – the grammar – go. Finally, the personality of the instructor often determines his or her philosophy of teaching grammar as much as anything else. But even the personality types seem to come in waves over the years, as do societal and political ideologies, reflected in the titles of college graduate courses and the philosophies of those teaching – and taking - them. Regarding grammar instruction, the pendulum continues to swing.

Patrick Hartwell makes the case that a teacher's view of grammar instruction dictates his or her view of "the issues of sequence in the teaching of composition and the role of the composition teacher" (108). In his "Grammar, Grammars, and the Teaching of Grammar", he maintains a decidedly partisan tone – but the disagreement centers on the *means* to an end. He "question[s] the value of teaching grammar" in the traditional teacher centered classroom with building block skills that lead to composition, but not the value of correctness itself (108). Primarily because so much of media and mainstream models of writing today do not model correctness ("u r lol"), it is imperative that teachers address grammar, along with purpose and audience and in the context of literacy and communication, in the classroom. A writing instructor may validate the students' own modes of composition - texting, social networking, blogging, emailing, gaming – and the language with which they communicate in these settings by not being critical of that language, but interested. Students can teach us to be successful in these modes and we can teach them standard academic English. It is not an affront to require it; it is not "old school". One does not dress for the beach or the dance, however cute he or she may be, the same way one dresses for an interview at the bank. Writing is the same. We must prepare students to succeed academically as well as socially.

Often we send mixed messages in the classroom regarding grammar instruction: "students are often drilled on the details of grammar or form and yet are forgiven for the minor mistakes they make in their writing . . . If the minor details weren't important in the end, why did the teachers spend so much time on them?" (Mori 135) Or, teachers spend no time on specific grammar instruction and then just expect students' writing to be stylistically correct. There are those instructors who will say "It's what you say, not how you say it." That is false. Writing is both. *How* one says something gives credibility and power, definition and authenticity, to *what* one says. It's true that grammar instruction for a while had a bad rap, and people insisted it could be done without the skill and drill, a reflection of the societal pendulum that equated such instruction with rigidity, authority, and discipline. And it's probably true that students rarely are able to connect drills and worksheets with their actual writing. Yet without the skill and drill, many teachers don't know how to address grammar at all, and end up editing papers instead of empowering students to edit their own work. So the question has to be addressed again: how do we best serve the needs of students regarding grammar instruction?

In practice, some teachers continue to advocate the traditional, linear skills and drills model. Particularly now with the public's attention so focused on test scores, "many [teachers] have turned to extensive low-level drill and practice sessions, leaving less time for students to read and write in authentic contexts" (Shosh and Zales). There are certain skills, teachers discover, that are generally on "the test," and we teach them. But most maintain that "writing" refers to composing and rhetorical choice, and that correctness of style can be taught more effectively through students' own writing. This error analysis, or building upon the skills the student already possesses while addressing mistakes as they arise in writing, is not a new concept, but was first proposed by Shaughnessy in 1977. It encourages students to write full-length essays, rather than engage in skill-and-drill exercises, to teach grammatical correctness. There is practical application of research to help teachers know how to approach error analysis, such as that reported on the Lehman College Faculty Resources web page entitled "Handling Surface Error in Student Writing." Instructors can identify *patterns* of error, which effectively allows the instructor to change the student's body of knowledge and avoid repeatedly acting as "editor". This often must be individualized: one student may lack understanding of the semi-colon; another, tense; still another, pronoun agreement. Rather than correcting or marking these errors, a five- minute intervention tutorial can change the student's thinking and knowledge base, thus enabling him to effectively edit his own paper. Instructors may restrict corrections to one paragraph, which again places the responsibility for editing, and therefore, learning to recognize error, on the student.

Another method of instructional feedback is simply a mark in the margin next to the line containing the grammatical error. Hartwell cites Richard H. Haswell who found that "his students correct 61.1% of their errors when they are identified with a simple mark in the margin rather than by error type." (121) A teacher may remark in the margin, to steal from Prose: "Is this grammatical?" If the teacher writes the more specific – "parallelism," for example – the student probably has no idea what it is and will ignore the comment or delete that part of the essay altogether, to be "safe", even if doing so detracts from his overall content and meaning. But he may be able to figure out the problem is and how to make the writing sound better, and thus, learn parallelism on his own, in the context of his own writing, without drill. If instead of inserting a semi-colon for a student in an essay, a teacher asks what is wrong with that sentence, most students can usually figure out the general problem and correct it, if not in the exact way that the teacher would have. This supports what Hartwell suggests: that poor writing is not always a "cognitive or linguistic problem, a problem of not knowing a 'rule of grammar', but rather . . . a problem of meta-cognition and meta-linguistic awareness, a matter of accessing knowledge" (Hartwell 121). But beware: although I have used this method successfully, initially I had parents and students unfamiliar with this teaching style complain that I did not correct the students' drafts, so how could they "make a good grade on the final draft?" It does not serve the students for a teacher to act as editor, yet that is what students expect and we as teachers get sucked into doing it time and again. Simply editing or correcting enables ignorance, where modeling and instruction facilitates knowledge, which in turn empowers and emancipates student writers. The aforementioned methods of error analysis prevent editing and encourage student ownership and learning.

There are curricular approaches that help writers employ conventions without understanding them. This is akin to rule memorization in math or spelling, such as "i before e except after c". Further, some approaches to grammar instruction only teach students to *recognize* conventions, by circling correct words, or proofreading and correcting errors in sentences; they never require students to *employ* the conventions in their own writing at all. When teachers tell students the "rules" but seldom require them to use these in writing and become familiar with how they work, we are missing the point, and "teaching to the test". Students will not understand any larger purpose in this type of instruction at all. It isn't meaningful. They aren't engaged, they aren't learning, and aren't growing as writers, which is the ultimate goal, or should be, of grammar instruction. An alternative technique is to use a combination of some drill and linear instruction, with active reading and writing assignments for application. As one example, instead of saying, "use 'whom' because it is the object of the preposition", and assigning worksheets which require students to circle who or whom in sentences, teachers may show them samples from texts in which authors have used these conventions, and give them assignments that require them to use who and whom repeatedly in their own writing. The Jane Austen exercise in chapter one provides a natural lesson in using the semi-colon.

When students are writing, they are more likely to see the purpose of grammar, to give them choices and to create and alter meaning of text. This same concept applies when teaching figurative language, and elements of style or rhetoric through reading. We must teach our students more than recognition of concepts, terms, techniques, and correct punctuation; we must teach application. Only then have we empowered anyone, really taught anyone, at all.

Teachers may use this method with a unit on words often confused. Students may learn the differences in words using workbooks first, and then write creative sentences and paragraphs using the words: complement/compliment; accept/except; desert/dessert; allusion/illusion; and so on. The same approach is effective with instruction in run-on sentences: instruct students in comma splices, conjunctive adverbs, conjunctions; then have them write sentences avoiding run-ons. Students can check each others' sentences, explaining why something is grammatically correct or not, and making it more likely students will actually learn because they are writing for an audience other than the teacher and interacting during the process. A good exercise and one that is fun for students is to study examples of text by authors who deliberately break the rules, and then allow the students to attempt to write this way themselves, to understand for what purposes and effects authors might use run-ons, or fragments. Students tend to think of *what* they say and *how* they say it as separate unless they are shown the relationship. Comments after teachers return essays with corrections in the margins might include: "So basically you're saying I'm a good writer, but I just don't get grammar, right?" and "So I would have made an A if I didn't have all these mistakes, because you liked my essay, right, you just counted off for grammar?" It doesn't serve the students to separate language from the composing process; it isn't even possible, really. There is the familiar parallel to human appearance: even though their character is what is on the inside (content), it is reflected in how they dress and present themselves (correctness of style). The two are not separate; together, they make up the whole person, or the whole essay. To be taken seriously in all walks of life and have all doors opened, enough to change their lives or someone's opinion or something in the world, students need to present the outside well. Teachers are so afraid of being critical of students' writing that we praise their ideas, examples, anything to give them positive feedback, reinforcing that grammar or correctness is separate from content. And yet, correctness – language - is the very thing that allows writers to make powerful meaning with the content. As the twelve- year old narrator insists in Barbery's *The Elegance of the Hedgehog*, "Grammar is a way to attain beauty". Grammatical savvy is empowerment for the writer, a useful tool in composition and not a separate skill.

When teachers fail to connect the various components, grammar included, of composition, we separate the mind from the spirit, the truth from the presentation of the truth, and it can't – shouldn't – be done. Kyoko Mori points out, interestingly, that in Japan, "there is no possibility that you can make a few minor mistakes and still 'get' the spirit or the essence of the 'truth' . . . In America, where teachers actually value the overall spirit of the work, they spend most of their time talking about details" (136). Indeed, just as detrimental to instruction as dismissing grammar altogether is giving feedback in such a way that perpetuates what some students already believe - that writing is all about the grammar. Teachers do this by focusing attention on small details without connecting them to the big picture. We do it in part because the details are something tangible and manageable; the spirit of writing, what makes a paper really amazing, is hard to articulate. Recently as I tutored students who had to pass an upcoming writing assessment, I found myself addressing and correcting errors in spelling, punctuation, sentence structure, and usage, because I was overwhelmed by the general writing issues: incorrect or inadequate attention to prompt, weak organization, no examples, no emotional impact. I didn't know where to start without having students begin completely again – and so, my initial inclination was to start with grammar. It's easier to articulate the "secondary things," believing that "what we value the most is beyond our meager ability to describe" (Mori 136). Applying the research about the reading/writing connection and the value of social interaction can enable students to get to the spirit, the value, that is within them, and that is hard for writing instructors to describe. Students need to understand what gives quality and meaning to literature, and that correctness of style is important as a means to that end, but is not an end in itself. If we specifically and primarily articulate and emphasize grammar and correctness, because it's something we can manage, we may produce writers who are good but not great, who can pass tests but not reach that next level as writers. However, it is a fine line; correctness of style lends credibility to writers' ideas and can cause them to be taken more seriously, which they desire. Teachers must give credence to both correctness and the "wow" factor, usually achieved by rhetorical choices, and voice. In proper order and with proper focus, some of the techniques of error analysis can help students improve both composition and style of their writing through that writing itself.

In addition to using the writing of the students themselves to teach grammatical correctness, the reading/writing connection can be a vital component of editing, and thus, writing instruction in general. Students may examine side by side their own writing and "models of academic prose" (Prose *Reading Like a Writer* 3) and compare such things as sentence structure, the use of gerunds, infinitives, parallelism, apostrophe, parenthesis, and quotation marks. This allows them to become more "conscious of style, of diction, of how sentences were formed . . . [they] discovered that writing, like reading, was done one word at a time, one punctuation mark at a time. It required . . . changing an adjective, cutting a phrase, removing a comma, and putting the comma back in." (Prose *Reading Like a Writer* 3) This "exposure to the code,"(i.e. good writing), through purposeful reading selections, is best practice (Hartwell 121). Stephen King insists that as a writer, "you have to learn the beat" (129). Students learn the grammar beat not by drill so much as by exposure, by reading, "feeling" it over and over. Lehman College agrees: "[Look] at an example of writing in your discipline and [notice] what the writer does. Are there certain conventions at work that make this a successful piece of writing?" In fact, the same passages given as examples of the reading connection in chapter one, or any passages from a teacher's own curriculum or textbook, can be used to teach grammatical correctness. But remember: it is not enough just to point to stylistic and grammatical choices; students must imitate these in their own writing. Cognition must become application to truly be banked by the students as knowledge to draw from later for all their writing needs as they arise. When writing like Austen, Steinbeck,

Hemingway, students will have to punctuate accordingly. They will learn how grammar in fact dictates meaning, and effect on readers – and learn to use that to their own benefit as writers. This more enjoyable and practical way of studying grammar has more lasting implications for students. In looking at samples of professional writing, perhaps students will realize that their essays are less "professional" because they are limited grammatically, and a better understanding of the conventions of correctness could lead to better writing, because "mastering the logic of grammar contributes . . . to the logic of thought" (Prose *Reading Like a Writer* 43). The reading-writing connection can be a powerful resource for grammar instruction.

Learning correctness, for those who did not grow up reading and writing, is akin to learning to do anything new for the first time. Uehling explains: "Acquiring grammar is like acquiring knowledge of a new city or learning a new software program – we learn what we need to know to carry out a purpose." When I think of the new technology I have had to learn and incorporate over the last several years in education, with regard to grades, accountability, transparency, lessons, curriculum – and all with regard to the computer – as a confirmed Luddite, I cringe. My students must feel the same way if correct grammar is as foreign to them as web pages, spread -sheets, and wikis were to me. The first thing I probably learned regarding technology was email – because I needed to get inter-office communications, and wanted to talk to my friends and family without calling them. Teaching writing is the same thing! These student writers are limited by a lack of prior knowledge and motivation - but once they see the new things that are available, and are encouraged to use them, they can do more advanced work and their enjoyment is greater.

If there is something they particularly want to communicate, their motivation to learn is greater. Students may need to practice skills and drills at times, but using their own writing and that of published writers is a way for them to see *why* they are practicing these skills. It is so much more fun and meaningful to locate the parts of speech or gerunds or fragments and run-ons in someone's story than in workbook sentences. And the more they actually write – like the more I use the computer – the less we will have to keep getting the manual out!

Prose reminds us that it is "essential to read great sentences . . . along with your style book" lest we get so caught up in the rules we forget our license to break them (*Reading Like a Writer* 44) Acquiring enough command to develop a voice is another benefit of improving grammar and usage through reading. It is hard to develop voice without consciously using, and sometimes breaking, the rules of grammar and usage. Style books teach what *not* to do in writing; great literature teaches affirmatively, by example. Hartwell, cites research as far back as 1893 that supports "active involvement with language [as] preferable to instruction in rules or definitions"(125). Isn't it time then to stop restating the same theories and confirming the same research and instead become committed to best practices in the classroom? "It is time that we, as teachers, formulate theories of language and literacy and let those theories guide our teaching" (Hartwell 127) Teachers should be using language to teach grammar, through the reading-writing connection and the students' own writing. This is yet another place the roads of successful writing instruction are not divergent but connected, and conveying that to students is a step toward meaningful and quality writing.

Acknowledging the social aspect of writing and the need for an authentic audience, as explained in chapter two, greatly improves correctness. In "Remedial Writers: the Teacher's Job as Corrector of Papers," Butler suggests that "the markings that a teacher puts on a basic writer's paper mean little . . . While the comments are meaningful to the instructor, they are not meaningful to the writer" (Adler-Kassner and Glau 87). I just almost fell over when I read this. I spend a lot of time commenting! But upon reflection, this statement is obviously true, and with some perspective, even amusing. My carefully constructed penciled comments on student papers are very likely the written version of Charlie Brown's teacher's voice; and all my students see (or hear) is "Blah, blah, blah, blah." My own classroom evidence supported the connection between providing social interaction with authentic audiences for writers and correctness of style. For an audience of their peers, in both formal and informal classroom activities, my students labored to word things exactly right. They questioned whether desired effects were achieved (most had never considered effects on the reader at all) and they struggled to achieve balance between appropriate language for academic writing and "keeping it real." In their non-fiction writing especially, having a peer group audience for their work seemed to validate not only their writing but also the experiences on which it was based. They were intrinsically motivated to revise and edit, which resulted in higher quality writing overall. The CCCC maintains that "language is always learned and used more effectively in environments where it accomplishes something the user wants to accomplish for particular listeners or readers within that environment" ("CCCC Writing Assessment: A Position Statement"). Revising and editing for a teacher on an assignment a student cares nothing about has little meaning to the student. Revising and editing on a state assessment has no authentic meaning – but if they have learned correctness previously, through a connected and meaningful instruction process, when they did have a real audience, they can recall and demonstrate enough prior knowledge to accomplish the purpose of the test. Using the reading-writing connection, visual representations of correctness, error analysis, and an authentic audience all may serve as motivation and access, and allow teachers to change their methods of grammar instruction without sacrificing that which is valuable in it.

Hartwell challenges: "At no point in the English curriculum is the question of power more blatantly posed than in the issue of formal grammar instruction" (127). Initially, I bristled at the negative connotation: "power," "blatantly," "formal." Upon reflection, why am I so defensive? Knowledge *is* power. Teachers have it. Students see grammar as a sort of esoteric language we speak that does not interest or involve them. ("btw"- they view text-speak as something that does not interest or involve us!) But in teaching, the goal is to transmit the power to the students, not withhold it. To be successful in teaching is akin to parenting: we want them to become independent, self-sufficient, and functioning, to fly the nest with the tools – the power – to succeed in the world. To transmit the power, we have to insist that students make connections. How many times have we drilled on a concept such as there/their and have our students perform perfectly on the skill and drill worksheet, only to make the very same error in their next writing assignment? They see the drill and writing as separate. Until they connect it, there is no improvement in writing whatsoever, which is the sole reason for the grammar instruction in the first place! In a sport, such as basketball, players learn the fundamentals for the obvious purpose of successfully playing the game. They don't regard the drills they do in practice for dribbling, passing, shooting, and defending the post as having naught to do with actually playing basketball, but as the foundation that will allow them to get more enjoyment out of the game. In fact, one can't play the game without some degree of skill. In the same way, students can learn to connect the rules and practice of grammar to writing and "demystify academic language" (Lehman). If I can learn to text – because I am motivated to do so and see the benefits to my lifestyle - they can learn to write standard academic English. They have to connect – to the reading, the purpose, the audience- so it matters to them that they choose correctly, that they gain and apply this power. They will learn to use the crossover dribble (comma) or the jump shot (active voice) in the big picture that is the offense (paragraph?) when circumstances dictate, because they care about winning the game or impressing their peers. Effective grammar instruction, in this same way, must be connected to the larger whole of effective writing instruction. At the same time, basketball players practice – a lot – and sometimes, this practice is on specific skills.

Teachers of high school English should be informed of the research on grammar instruction. Read a lot of it to see how and why theories were formed. Decide what consistent practices will offer composing and editing abilities that are meaningful enough to students to be remembered and applied. Employing various methods of error analysis, reading for a study of language, interacting with peers and a meaningful audience, and writing, writing, writing are all solid ways to effectively incorporate grammar instruction into the writing classroom. "Being correct is not an end in itself" (Mori 142) but it is a means to an end, and one that we as writing instructors have responsibility to provide. Some emphasize it less and are less comfortable teaching it, but I agree with Shaughnessy: "It is irresponsible to tell [the student] that correctness is not important…it is not impossible to give him the information and practice he needs to manage his own proofreading" (11). Accountability in presentation is not going away, in academic or real world communities.

CHAPTER FOUR

Politics

My message to share
To this world
Is to press through what you can not do – fear
If you despise heights – then get on a mountain top
If you can't swim – then try and learn
If you have a physical disability – then find out how to do it –
Your way
If you got dyslexia – then read and write

Do not let the world bring you down
Do not let fears bring you down
Take what you cannot do and do it
To prove you can
- Jessica Etheridge, 16, dyslexic

ONE OF MY INITIAL IDEAS FOR A book was a conservative manifesto on education that would address teacher efficacy in the face of constant philosophical, pedagogical and political shift in areas of teaching writing to "alphabet kids"(referring to the labels given to special education students), English language learners, and "basic writers". The book would promote meaningful, authentic teaching, feedback, and evaluation; and attack the "dummying down" that results when culture and politics dictate instruction. What I found, though, was consistent with *all* writing instruction: when the goal of most teachers, students and writers is to make a difference rather than to merely make a statement, the superfluous is shed and best practices for writing instruction can be applied across the lines of culture and ability.

There are few fields in the constant state of flux, or under constant siege, as education. In recent years much conversation among English instructors, has focused on the concept, instruction, and assessment of "basic writers". And so I have found myself wondering how and why the phrase and course "basic writing" came to be necessary. Why was it suddenly important that I have as part of my Masters Degree, a course with this distinction? Years ago students who struggled with writing stayed after class, with the instructor, or in labs or writing centers, or with an actual tutor that the student himself took the responsibility to acquire when he realized he needed help in the course. Are there more basic writers now than before, so that now it is warranted to have basic writing as a separate discipline, a separate course, as a topic *separate* from teaching English? And if so, doesn't that speak to a larger, societal issue that has bled into academia, providing a basis for the "conservative sentiment toward public education"? (McNenny 3) Do we need a basic writing course prerequisite in college because high school standards for graduation are lower now? "No child left behind" sounds good in theory, but in practice hasn't it come to mean easier course work and lower grading standards, with allowances made for age, an alphabet label, a minority or disability or "social location"? Do we require students to master certain skills to receive credit, and are the skills the same as they were twenty years ago? I have heard that a Master's Degree is the new Bachelor's, as more people are accessing higher education, which is a good thing – unless it isn't that people have aspired to more, but that higher education standards have just changed to include more people. Does a college degree mean what it used to? Are university and graduate school entrance requirements easier now so more students can get in? *Why?* And to be even more blunt: Are we dumber now, or lazier? More tolerant, or less moral? *What have we done?*

One thing it appears to me we have done is created this entity known as "basic writing." There are many who ask the same questions I have posed. "Basic writing programs are targeted as being symptomatic of a tolerance for underachievement and continued support for the failed liberal support programs, much like welfare and other 'entitlement' programs for the poor." (McNenny, preface xiii). It is fashionable to take basic yoga, and basic cooking, but there is an assumption that writing ought to have been learned early in life, and that failing to do so indicates that something is not right – with motivation, with education, with ability. Teaching writing to struggling students is not a new concept. Everything is just more transparent now, in an age of accountability. Every weakness is a mark against a teacher, a school. As long as there have been hieroglyphics there have been basic writers, and those who have unlocked the mystery to teach them. It was done routinely as part of education without all the mystery, labels, politics and discourse getting in the way. All of education was something people worked hard – and some harder than others - to achieve. So is separating, naming and/or practicing the teaching of "basic writing" – and the macrocosmic it represents - a service to the world community, or a disservice?

All the politics about basic writing instruction are moot in the face of accountability, "when students in special education programs are held to the same standard of achievement in academic development as regular education students" (Fu and Shelton). It brings to the forefront for teachers what the students have always known: that they need to be able to write. Language "works, in communicating meaning, precisely because its elements are conventional among users" (Bernstein *Teaching Developmental Reading* 21). So why would we excuse or accept language use in academia that is not standard: not coherent, not cohesive, and not correct? Indeed, "it is cold comfort to a student who is not doing well" that his failure is due to a disability (White). This brings us back to the premise that good writing instruction is invaluable and available for all students in all areas of academia. There are many reasons some students may struggle more than their peers with writing, and instructors need to be aware of these. Some writers are overwhelmed with things outside their knowledge base or comfort zone: terminology, types of reading assignments and use of the computer. Specific basic writing instruction can serve as a buffer for older students returning to college, a way to ease back into academic life. At the high school and college level, teachers serve students with language barriers, some for whom English is a second or third language. Educators have referred to this population as ESL (English as a Second Language) and/or ELL (English Language Learner). And we serve students with learning disabilities, from mild to severe, who are trying to learn with the "mainstream". We teach those whom Uehling asserts make up the two types of basic writers: those who have surface level grammar, structure, and style deficits, and those whose content is weak, vague, or trite. However it is defined, writing instruction has levels of progression like any instruction; requires motivation (provided by audience and interest) and access (provided by making connections of reading to writing and studying models of correctness); and is improved, like any skill, with much practice. There is research to inform teachers specifically in areas of mainstreamed special education students and English language learners, which is worth consideration.

Mainstreaming is a term used in many high schools to delineate the practice of teaching students with learning disabilities or disadvantages in the regular classroom. How many of those are in the regular classroom depends largely on the federal, state, and local politics at the time. In recent years, and in part as a result of "No Child Left Behind" legislation, there has been a push to exit students from special education programs into the regular classroom. Most of these students have minimal writing skills and are well below the level of their peers, making them "basic writers". Right now I have students who read several grades below level, whose low IQ scores do not qualify them as learning disabled, who speak English as a second or third language, or who suffer from dyslexia or Attention Deficit Disorder or something else, in the regular classroom with students for whom learning comes easily. The idea behind the legislation is that when challenged, these disadvantaged students will rise to the level of those around them. Throw a non-swimmer in the lake and say sink or swim. He may realize he is drowning, and flail around enough to save himself for a time. Throw a basic writer in and say sink or swim. But he has no arms and legs, and he may not even realize he is disabled. It's nice to say he will rise to the level of the writers (or swimmers) around him; it is more probable that he will be intimidated by them, or drown. The classroom teacher must be informed of instructional strategies to best meet the urgent needs of these students.

Mainstreaming works with much one on one tutoring by the teacher; the swimmer wouldn't drown if the lifeguard were out there in the water, helping only him. Indeed, these students need a support system beyond what time constraints allow the classroom teacher. Content mastery, learning labs, writing workshops, whatever name is current for providing support instruction and practice in high schools should resemble what Marti Singer advocates: reinforcing the students' actual classroom assignments and helping them with those instead of doing separate skills or adding assignments to already struggling writers. ("Moving the Margins") But if this support is in a separate environment with an instructor other than the classroom teacher, as is often the case, these teachers also need to be well informed of the terminology, expectations, assignments, and philosophy of the English department's writing program. The classroom teacher, department chair, or campus writing expert should meet with the special education teachers and aids, and everyone who will be working with students on assignments they receive in the regular classroom. This type of training and communication assures that all involved are all on the same page with regard to writing instruction. These support teachers should have: a list of terms associated with the writing process; a basic writing format, rubric and checklist; the various stages and steps of the writing process as it will be practiced in the classroom; samples of reading selections and student writing that model end-goals of a writing assignment and correctness of stylistic or rhetorical choices; and specific surface errors that will be addressed. Communication between teachers should be frequent as students are working on assignments to ensure that all are aware in what area the students need reinforcement, and what errors are being specifically targeted on a certain assignment or for an individual student. These instructors also need training on error analysis for grammar instruction, so they do not simply edit for the students whom they assist. Content Mastery, or a Learning Lab, is a place mainstreamed English students can really improve on their writing with much needed one-on-one instruction, if these instructors are adequately equipped.

I would take a further step and say if an English teacher is the writing expert on campus and has strategic knowledge about teaching writing to the special education or ELL population, it would benefit the students for that information to be shared across the curriculum with *all* instructors on campus. If teachers have these types of conversations and then apply consistent knowledge and expectations throughout campus, students will come to understand that writing well is a lifetime skill required for communication, and not just something isolated in the English classroom an hour a day. This method of Content Mastery and cross-curricular support for these basic writers, combined with best practices in the classroom environment, allows for differences in learning styles and abilities, provides intensive individual instruction and reinforcement, and assures consistency in writing instruction and expectations for the student from instructor to instructor throughout the school day, creating a more authentic educational experience. But what are these "best practices" for instructing basic or struggling writers in the actual classroom?

The first thing teachers have to do is "unlearn classroom practices that underestimate student writers" (Shosh and Zales). One wonders why teaching fragmented skills is so often recommended for students with Learning Disabilities, when the research indicates that it is not the best method, for teaching writing or reading to anyone. Likewise, focusing on deficits in students' writing only emphasizes what they *cannot* do while restricting the scope of creativity and rhetorical choices, things which may represent potential for success in other areas of the writing process. Thomas Reynolds and Patrick Bruch denounce "Developmental writing programs [which] have traditionally offered instruction 'from the ground up' by asking students to master what are often seen as smaller, more manageable units of writing, such as the sentence, before moving on to tackle longer, more involved writing projects." They disprove the "assumption that students will be less frustrated and make better progress if they first learn the 'building blocks' of writing and then make use of them in writing courses that ask for more complex pieces of writing." Especially as students get older, they are going to be bored and frustrated with these "building blocks" that they perceive have no meaning and connection to their own lives. Even with intensive instruction, basic writers can do pages of worksheets on sentence patterns or prepositional phrases, repeatedly get more than half of them wrong, miss them again on the test, have no idea why they are doing them, and show no improvement whatsoever in writing. They see no connection at all between the worksheets and the desired written outcome. Why then, would a teacher keep assigning these activities when the writing – the goal of grammar instruction, after all – does not improve?

Holistic teaching works better, and requires less "accommodations" because students are not focused on each inadequacy or struggle but on the whole situation, *one in which they have an interest.* The interest has been developed through choice in reading selections and writing responses to those selections, social interaction during the process, and an authentic audience. At the risk of sounding repetitive, it's like everything else in life:

I have to *care* how to work the navigation system on the car to read the manual. Many struggling writers hate school. If instead of having them write on a subject of interest to them, with specific purpose and a real audience, I have them do workbook sentences or respond to a canned prompt to which they feel no connection, they will not care if they write anything or not. I took Calculus in high school until one day it hit me: when on Earth was I going to need Calculus in my life? Well, these basic writing students often view grammar (correctness), especially when taught to them in isolated fashion, in the exact same way, and not as an important component of writing, or literacy. In fact, they don't even see writing as an important component of their lives. It is a non-factor to them. And they fail at it, which adds to their discomfort and mistrust. So the theory is, we need to give these students meaningful, holistic assignments. Then what?

Reynolds and Bruch found that when students understand the context in which literacy operates they "came to see conventions of correctness in new and more meaningful ways". They quote a student who claims to have finally gained understanding of "why a way of writing is right – and why it is wrong," and another who stated: "At the beginning of the year I was able to write a basic paper following a certain format. At the end, I could write a paper with the correct content and vary the style in which it was written." (Reynolds and Bruch) This occurred because the students could see the whole picture- they made connections between the writing form and their own developmental rhetorical choices. Teachers should not be too quick to oppose use of a form, or rubric to help ELL students and mainstreamed students feel like they have some direction and control. Purposeful holistic writing with a format to guide students is a more effective teacher of all components of the writing process than sentence exercises and fragmented skills tests. In addition to helping many special education, ELL, or basic writers, a writing formula may help others as well: students who love math and are good at it but struggle with the abstract components of writing; students who just need direction and are afraid of writing initially, possibly because of bad experiences or failure in the past; and students who are creative and elaborative writers but who lack cohesiveness and tend to digress way too much for some academic writing. A form can be as specific as dictating each sentence that makes up a paragraph: topic sentence, fact, quote, support, support, fact/quote, support, support, and concluding sentence. (This is a popular model; terms and vocabulary may vary from teacher to teacher or state to state, but most writing instructors recognize the intent and purpose of each "label" even if they call it something different.) Students can even label the sentences, following a specific rubric or form for each sentence in a paragraph and each paragraph in an essay, to learn how to organize their writing and not be overwhelmed by a blank page. I tell my students it's not the Bible; they won't go to hell if they get off the beaten path. In fact, the road to Heaven is wide in writing; there are lots of ways to get through those gates. (Just look at our earlier example of Hemingway and Faulkner's tone and style.) Teachers may want to take a more general approach to form, giving students the parts of an essay and some broad questions on a rubric so they can self-check and reorganize if they need to:

*Do you have a good lead-in and a clear thesis in the intro?

*Is paper divided into fairly balanced paragraphs?

*Do paragraphs have topic sentences and concluding sentences that tie everything together so readers don't get lost in examples?

*Did you check for specific surface errors we recently emphasized in class?

*Did you read aloud for cohesiveness?

*Do paragraphs have good balance between facts or quotes and elaboration?

For students who are have an intrinsic fear of writing, or those basic writers who have difficulty managing the many aspects of the process at once, a form lessens apprehension and can at least introduce them to writing, as one component of instruction, and I have had great success with it.

Amber was a basic writer mainstreamed into my classroom from special education for the first time as an 11th grader. She had never passed a state writing assessment test, and often just left the essay- writing portion of the test blank, repeating to instructors that she couldn't think of anything to say about the topic. Amber could never seem to just get started putting something on paper. She was thrilled to have a writing format, which I provided initially, because it took away her tremendous fear and gave her a place to start, sentence by sentence. She used it religiously. As she progressed as a writer, I explained to her the purpose and idea behind the format -- what the topic sentence actually does for the reader, how to choose her facts and quotes, how to use elaboration. I showed her, through literature and other students' works, how and why most writers adhere to the premise behind the form of a paragraph, if not the actual exact form, and gradually, Amber began to understand, and as she gained more experience -- and confidence - writing real paragraphs and essays using her formula, she began to make small, stylistic choices that deviated from the form. She began to see writing in the context of communication, as something she could do. Because of this, she began to ask me – and other students – about specific editing issues in her text. She still struggles with academics: she rarely passes a grammar worksheet or multiple- choice exam, can't label parts of speech or sentences or circle the correct verb in practice sentences, and gets nervous when confronted with timed writing assignments in isolated settings. She may not pass a state assessment with contrived multiple- choice questions and answers about grammar, or reading comprehension passages. But Amber's last real writing project was organized, developed, cohesive, interesting, and almost error-free – and she completed all stages of the process, including editing – herself. She may always use that form (she memorized it) as a starting point when faced with a writing challenge; but it is better than not being able to write at all. Primarily, she gained confidence, and thus began to develop as a writer, when nothing else had worked for years. This type of holistic instruction – starting with the writing and breaking it down to a formula, like error analysis – can work if teachers instruct in the components of the form and the correction of errors *in context of literacy*, and not just list or edit for the students. Teachers may include drilling within the context of the larger assignment, such as working on a specific part of the form or surface errors - gathering evidence, lead-in or thesis, concluding sentences, sentence structure - *as long as it is connected* to a larger purpose in which students can invest. Meaningful instruction is bigger than teaching basic writing, or LD, or any one discipline at all.

In response to overwhelming evidence that the linear, skill based instruction is not effective with mainstreamed special education students or regular education students, several teachers have conducted their own experiments. One such study is reported by Danling Fu and Nancy Shelton, who sought to allow for the social and emotional growth of all students without ignoring accountability in a writing workshop which emphasized social interaction and peer response, good literary models, and identifiable goals and improvements for surface correctness in order to achieve meaning. "With the writing workshop model, the teacher helps students to develop their writing concepts and skills by providing time, direct instruction, and one-on-one coaching; with only rare exceptions, all students improve from one piece of writing to another." (Fu and Shelton) My own "experiment" in an after school writing workshop with a group of students who were mainstreamed into my regular education English classroom during the day supported these findings. I allowed them to sit where they wanted, and noticed that they grouped themselves with peers with whom they would be comfortable sharing their writing. They responded verbally to prompts first, without my suggesting it, sharing in small group conversations that often digressed well beyond what I believed the prompt entailed. They wanted each other to check their work constantly: "Can I read you my intro?" and "Is this a good start?" They asked each other about spelling, and vocabulary: "What is a better word for this?" Periodically I talked to the students about direction, purpose, creativity, or organization. I tried to point out good rhetorical choices that they should repeat, and only focused on a couple of surface level things at a time. These were often different for each student, but inevitably, those seated nearby didn't have the same issues, and they helped each other. The ELL student who did not put endings on verbs – his verbs were never plural, never past tense – was seated next to the special education student whose entire page of writing was a run-on sentence. Another student who could never remember any prior experiences to use for examples sat by a dyslexic student who had dozens of examples for everything but could not spell "example" if her life depended on it. All students benefited by this arrangement and instruction; their writing improved, and though some of them were in forced attendance, they actually enjoyed the workshop. These activities are consistent with all writing instruction, but even more necessary and effective with mainstreamed and English language learner students, *who are more dependent on the choices the teacher makes for their learning* than their regular education peers. Within the realm of holistic instruction, best practices can be adjusted and implemented to meet the needs of these "basic" writers.

One mistake many teachers make with basic writers is taking things for granted, assuming too much prior knowledge. This is akin to purchasing a new appliance or furniture item that says "easy assembly" on the box – and since it is so "easy" there are certain terms or tools the originator takes for granted we are familiar with, and we are not. This is most frustrating for me with technology, and probably the reason the little techie at the cell phone store hides in the back when he sees me coming. The strategy of error correction, while a good one, often makes use of grammatical and rhetorical terminology with which basic writers are unfamiliar. As established in chapter three, when students don't understand a comment, they just ignore that suggestion or delete that part of the essay. This is especially true for basic writers, for whom manageable structure and feedback are so important. The key is "manageable". We must avoid being the proverbial bull with the comments on students' writing. "Teachers should not mark an excessive number of errors or correct errors that haven't yet been taught. Instead, they should identify one or two skill deficit areas at a time and teach those skills" (Scott and Vitale "Teaching the Writing Process to Students with LD"). Tell the student his run-ons are keeping readers from understanding how to read his paper. Explain what needs to be on each side of a semi-colon and let him correct and work on that one area for a while. Don't let him just avoid the semi-colon because he is unsure how to use it; have him experiment and use it in every paragraph. Equally important as the amount and quality of instructor feedback, is that students see the conventions of correctness as part of a context within which literacy operates – that the aspects of writing are not mutually exclusive. (Reynolds and Bruch) Run-on sentences are not to be avoided simply because it is "the law" but because they obscure meaning. I am a smart person, but no one would know this by my cell phone deficiency. If I knew how to use half the features on that phone, I would be able to perform many tasks in one place that now require me to consult various sources in multiple locations. I am limited in what I can do only because I just don't care all that much; I don't see a connection to my quality of life. Could this be what is limiting so many of our students? Teach grammar, correctness, all of the conventions of standard academic English as these may help the writers carry out tasks that matter to them. Students must first desire, for whatever reason, to want to write well; then have access and understanding of the tools required for assembly.

Using the computer, with spell or grammar check engaged, to write, while enjoyable for many students, reinforces the notion that the correct use of the conventions of writing and the quality of what one has to say are one and the same. It's hard to write when green and red lines appear on every sentence. Talk about being the bull – or bully! It's hard for experienced writers to ignore these automatic insults; basic writers are completely distracted and overwhelmed by them, often losing their entire thought process trying to figure out what is wrong with the last sentence. Sometimes, they forget what the prompt was or what they were even writing about! To them, writing *is* convention. They can't separate it. Red and green mean they are bad writers, that they are doing something wrong. They get so frustrated by this one aspect of the writing process that it limits – and ruins – the entire experience. "The complex process of writing poses many challenges for students with LD. They usually possess only basic writing skills and cognitive deficits and tend to be less aware of all five stages of the writing process [planning, drafting, revising, editing, publishing]." (Scott and Vitale "Teaching the Writing Process to Students with LD") At the computer these students enter the editing stage with the first sentence, and never freely plan, draft, or revise. To focus these basic writers on the entire composing process rather than this "edit as you write" mentality, teachers should model all of the stages for the students: show them various methods of planning and drafting ideas, or engage in free writing; have them group similar ideas from the planning stage together for potential paragraphs, and communicate with peers about them; check for support for main ideas, in the form of examples, elaboration, quotes or research if necessary. Print drafts of the work in progress and show them, complete with typographical or other errors, how a writer may move paragraphs, delete or add sentences, draw arrows with pencil, rearrange, reword, check sources – all without ever acknowledging surface or grammatical errors at all. Remember:

focusing feedback on *what* the basic writers say initially is more important than focusing on *how* they say it, or they won't say anything with any depth or complexity at all. Therein lies the danger of having basic writers draft on the computer, unless they can write and revise initially without the editing mechanisms engaged. There is a time and place for editing, particularly as doing so will contribute to meaning, clarity, effectiveness, and style. Students will learn in small steps to improve the method (correctness) when they begin to see that doing so does improve the message (content), but not until they have at least developed that message. The computer grammar and spell check provide a certain type of feedback, and teachers know all feedback is critical. It can help a basic writer grow, or kill what enthusiasm for writing was present.

A conversation about English language learners always turns political. In America it is politically correct to expect everyone to adjust to the needs of all citizens – and even, sometimes, those who aren't citizens. Virginia Crisco suggests students should be taught in their home languages and to their own needs. However, according to the National Commission on Writing's report on a survey of business leaders:

> writing is a 'gatekeeper' – an observation with implications for English language learners, for unless our society pays attention to developing all of the education skills (including writing) of all segments of the population, it runs the risk of consigning many students who are poor, members of minority groups, or learning English to relatively low-skill, low-wage, hourly employment. (VanDeWeghe)

As a writing instructor, I am not responsible for developing "processes for activism through writing"(Crisco 56). I am responsible for providing motivation, access and instruction that will benefit all students in academic and world environments. As an educator, a writing instructor, it is my job and not the army's to ensure that my students can "be all they can be." I assume the students being educated in America want to enter into this mainstream and be successful. Likewise, as students grow and change, their agendas, needs and goals will. I cannot just prepare college composition students for a certain task or workforce, or high school students to just pass the state assessment because their current agendas do not include higher education or an academic career. Why would I limit them in that way? I must see beyond the students' present into their futures. Crisco calls an initiative that states "all children in CA public schools should be taught English..." assimilation; and criticizes "laws that force students to learn English in public institutions..." (44). Gloria Anzaldua agrees, lashing out at her primary school's English only policy, and at being given required additional English instruction in college (as quoted in Bernstein, *Teaching Developmental Reading* 302). On the contrary, such legislation serves the students' long-term goals. I would contend that it is actually my responsibility as a teacher to help the student assimilate the language correctly. Anzaldua "may not have agreed with some of the outcomes of those language policy decisions, yet it is notable that she has achieved well developed skills with written English that have allowed her to be successful academically and professionally in American culture as a result" (Bernstein *Teaching Developmental Reading* 10). Right now, I have a student who has been in this country two years and struggles desperately with the language. Her limited vocabulary limits her reading and writing ability. She wants to stay here, where a girl can graduate from high school, go to college, and embark on a career path. This country is very competitive and I would do her a disservice if I replaced her academic rigor with excuses. I may find a different bridge by which she can cross, and we may travel more slowly, but I must get her to the same place. Consideration for language difficulties is not the same as making excuses for them, and it does not sacrifice a long-term destination simply because the journey is hard. People cannot insist that becoming "Americanized" is not a "valued goal" (Crisco 49) when it's hard or uncomfortable, such as in education, while at the same time embracing the freedoms, advantages and benefits, and hoping to enter the job market this country offers. If business leaders maintain that writing is a gatekeeper, my responsibility as a writing instructor to distribute keys is huge. Excuses and political indignation do not empower people to live the lives they have imagined. Access does.

June Jordan did not just advocate acceptance of Black English in college classrooms, she actually taught it as a course. ("Nobody Mean More to Me than You and the Future Life of Willie Jordan"). Furthermore, her class, mobilized around an African American classmate whose brother was killed by white policemen in Brooklyn, New York, wrote letters to the police department in Black English. I can understand writing in Black English intentionally in a course to achieve voice or dialect. I can agree that an understanding of it is necessary to study and appreciate some literature. But instead of teaching "The Art of Black English" as a semester long course for college credit, why not teach a course that unravels *many* of the different varieties of the English language, or examines various cultures at work in the writing process? I understand *why* her students wrote to the police department in the dialect they did: "making basic writing a political act can create opportunities for students and instructors to examine what literacy is, why it is defined as it is, and what it might be for the future" (Adler-Kassner and Harrington 12). I am just not sure it was the mature, responsible, most effective choice *to make a difference*, if that is in fact what they were trying to do, which is not the same as *making a statement*. A balance must be struck in the classroom that depends largely on where and what the goals are. It is good to help all students find *what* to write, in various languages and backgrounds – but *how* to write is still determined by audience and purpose. Call it "publication location," rather than social location. Students in the course in Black English may have become more politically aware. But did they become better writers? Will that instruction allow them to more effectively enter the conversations around them, or move an audience? Writing instruction must move beyond the cultural studies and politics of the 70s and 80s, just as it has moved beyond the singular skill-and-drill grammar approach of the 50s and 60s. We do not serve our English language learners socially, academically, or professionally, by indulging them in political correctness.

In contrast, Kay Thurston explains in "Mitigating Barriers to Navajo Students' Success in English Courses" how instructors at Navajo Community College on the Navajo reservation in Arizona address tangible concerns of budget, family obligations, attendance, and audience while providing access for their students to the academic community (Thurston). Educating teachers about whom they are teaching is a good practice, and in my own experience, gets good results. Otherwise we are teaching curriculum and not people. "Second language writers often come from contexts in which writing is shaped by linguistic and cultural features different from their NES peers" ("CCCC Statement on Second Language Writing and Writers"). On the reservation, with 96% Navajo, this awareness and adjustment are easier to do than in most inner city community colleges and public high schools. In my own classroom the students for whom English is a second language have varying home languages, backgrounds and attitudes about education and writing. Still, like Kay Thurston at NCC, I must have *strategies* to address their academic writing deficiencies, rather than saying the rest of the world just has to accept that the students' cultures are different and therefore they must be allowed to write differently. If writing is a gatekeeper, then there are not multiple keys to open the doors to academia and the work place. Standard Academic English (SAE) by definition is, for the most part, still standard. Bernstein agrees with goals and methods that "produce better results in helping bilingual and second language/dialect students achieve literacy and writing skills so that they can attain their objectives for participating in the educational system" (*Teaching Developmental Reading*). Basic writing courses at NCC deal with problems specific to Navajo students, and the kinds of errors they make, using Navajo themes and special textbooks. This is congruent with the CCCC Statement on Second Language Writing and Writers: writing instructors must have knowledge of the community to assess fairly a writer from that community; and tests that focus on what is grammatically or stylistically wrong instead of rhetorical choices misrepresent the abilities of students of color. Instructors should "approach SAE as one dialect, not superior... but the *one required for success* in the world..." (Thurston). Our own political beliefs, or our students', about that requirement are not relevant. A 2005 survey conducted by the National Writing

Project found that writing well improves career advancement for all employees, and the National Commission on Writing report on employment and promotion concurs (VanDeWeghe). "Here in the Southwest, then, effective instructors would teach *both* the Western and the Navajo rhetorical styles, privileging neither, and would explain *the necessity of taking audience and purpose into account when choosing...*" (Thurston, my italics). This college is respectfully making a difference for its students. It is serving them responsibly, putting real student needs above political agendas. If we want to *make a statement*, we can allow students to exist on whatever cultural island they want and demand that the rest of the world accept them where they are. If we want to *make a difference*, we must bridge the gap between the cultures and written expression through understanding and preparation.

The authors of *Basic Writing as a Political Act* bemoan the "school success narrative" and the "iconic student figures": Should we "portray literacy as an objective set of strategies and skills that can be mastered by iconic student figures with the drive and determination necessary?" (Adler-Kassner and Harrington 80) They question the very premise that the instructional theory and strategies in this book should apply to *all* students, complaining that schools seek to "ensure that students have mastered these objective skills, and that these skills also reflect a set of values and will help students to enter a middle-class culture that also participates in them" (69). Isn't that the goal of a writing instructor, or any teacher or mentor – to inspire, inform, and equip students to enter their futures as self-sufficient and capable of success in their chosen careers or academia? And common sense dictates that students must participate; they must take some ownership and responsibility for their own education. There are those who would suggest that "basic writing students…cannot use this system to advance their situations and participate in the dominant culture" (Adler-Kassner and Harrington 72). Why not? Is it better to relegate them to low-wage jobs and an inability to write well for all purposes? These authors are not crediting the college students they are referring to in this text, who apparently are skilled enough to get into college, with the ability to learn the skills taught there. They want to change the skills – the requirements – of academia so all can participate, instead of changing the paradigms and pedagogy in the approach to instruction. This is "No Child Left Behind" at the university level. I'd love to play professional golf, but I don't expect the LPGA to change the qualifying score for me, or make the cup bigger on the green so I can putt with more success, or eliminate bunkers because I do not do well from them. If I hired a skilled golf professional as an instructor, I would expect to be taught in the very best, most sound and current method available, and I would still expect to have to work very hard at it. This reverse discrimination, and I contend it *is* discrimination – of accepting lower quality or changing standards altogether does not serve English language learners but hinders them and is a step backward for society. It is detrimental at both the high school level and the college level. What the public – and the research - has to say about writing is important for *all* students. The standards of academic literacy and communication, as much as possible, should be accessible to all students, not altered for them.

Those who do not want English language learners to have to learn and use correct Standard Academic English believe that "asking students to abandon their culture outside of the classroom door so that they can more ably use that language can be damaging" (Adler-Kassner and Harrington 80). No one is asking students to abandon anything. The classroom does not define them. The entire school curriculum does not define them, any more than it defines the teacher. As instructors and students we have plenty of opportunities to enjoy our culture outside of school and certainly it remains with us as we go through school and all areas of our lives. It colors everything we think and say and do, and who we are. A person of a certain faith doesn't check his faith at the door of a secular classroom. He doesn't have to talk about it every minute for it to be valid. The same is true of culture and home language. Students are encouraged to "bring the languages, experiences, and images of their home communities into the classroom to be used as resources in service of student learning" (Van Deweghe, quoting from the National Writing Commission's reports). In fact, an instructor might enjoy asking ELL students how they write things correctly in their home languages. It provides a greater understanding of the patterns of errors and governing paradigms in their writing. A discussion of home language can elicit insight and compassion and be most interesting; but it must be practical and not political, and serve the needs of students as applies to writing instruction, or it belongs in cultural studies or political science class. Our society and its education system, and our students, could benefit from less concern about political correctness and more about correctness. All students still need "access to academic knowledge" (Reynolds and Bruch).

The NCTE/CCCC advocates that writing assessments should be sensitive to culture, race, class, gender and disabilities of student writers. They aren't. We as instructors must not fail them as well through "prescriptive attitudes toward language and discourse form, coupled with a certain inability to help students acquire standard written grammar"(Bernstein *Teaching Development Reading*). We have to prepare these students for the tests they need to pass to gain entrance to the world – be it college, career, graduation. So, there must be some method to this madness, which is significant when having those political discussions about English language learners or No Child Left Behind or Black English. Within best practices already defined, there are specific techniques effective for ELL students. "To reduce the risk of evaluating students on the basis of their cultural knowledge rather than their writing proficiency, students should be given several writing prompts to choose from when appropriate" ("CCCC Statement on Second Language Writing and Writers"). Choice ensures that students have experiences on which to draw for content. Particularly when instructors are not familiar with a student's home language or culture, choice reduces the risk of evaluating a student's knowledge of idioms, cultural themes, or vocabulary instead of the writing. In addition, students may be asked to reword or verbalize a writing prompt in their home language, identifying clearly what is being asked of them and what their response would be; they can then negotiate more effectively the rhetorical choices for academic English after thinking it through in their home language. This works with the short answer questions on many state assessments as well as essays and longer writing assignments. The "balanced approach [to writing instruction], one that seeks mastery of both content and form, requires attention to both process and product" is "especially beneficial to language minority students whose home dialect or home language is not Standard American English, and who struggle in school as a result" yet "need access to a well-rounded version of English". (Hagemann). The students may get the answer (on short answer assessments) right first; then make the answer clear to readers. They may identify what they have to offer to the conversation about the prompt given on a writing assignment or assessment; then make that interesting and entertaining for readers, through clarity, which is achieved by rhetorical choice and correctness. "Second language students may require more conferencing time with their teachers, so that teachers can discuss global issues first, and then attend to local issues" ("CCCC Statement on Second Language Writing and Writers"). Likewise as they formulate essays, particularly in the planning stages, second language students may benefit from attending to the global first, in their home language, and the local, or surface – the presentation - second.

Just as with mainstreamed students, the amount of grammatical and usage errors in the writing of ELL students can be overwhelming and cause instructors to miss what the students actually have to say. It helps to realize that initially, until access through instruction is provided, these are *language* differences and not stylistic errors. "Mono-lingual, mono-cultural instructors who lack knowledge about the world's major languages are likely to view the by-products of the cultural and linguistic knowledge of their second language students that appear in their English composition as mistakes, which they then set out to correct" (Bernstein *Teaching Development Reading*). These students, according to Yu Ren Dong, in "The Need to Understand ESL Students' Native Language" are actually struggling "to adapt to a new discourse in the new culture" and "instead of treating these different ways of knowing as deficient" we as teachers could plan our instruction to be "responsive to their needs" (Bernstein, *Teaching Developmental*

Reading). Knowing that language differences are not "errors" makes the idea of instructing these students much less daunting, and more exciting – it is code breaking, really! Feedback for second language writers should be individualized:

> Teacher preparation should include discussion on how the prose second language writers produce can violate their aesthetic expectations for academic English; instructors, instead, should look for the textual features that are rhetorically effective, and prioritize two or three mechanical or stylistic issues that individual second language writers should focus on throughout the duration of the course" ("CCCC Statement on Second Language Writing and Writers").

My students from Tahiti, Mexico, and Montenegro do not need the same surface level or mechanical instruction; they make vastly different "errors" and even have a different set of governing beliefs in their approach to writing for an audience. Just this extra attention to prompt, social interaction with peers, feedback, individual conferencing and assessing, and focusing on surface level errors unique to the individual writer helps second language learners adapt more quickly to standard academic English.

Whether as a separate entity or part of the regular curriculum, basic writing instruction has always been a component of teaching English. Politics and personal agendas and interests aside, research-based best practices in the writing classroom prepare all students to succeed. Teachers do not get to make judgments about whether special education, at-risk, ELL or any students should be mainstreamed into our classrooms. We do not get to decide whether requiring standard academic English for English language learners is the right thing, or whether we are discriminating by not allowing Black English or Spanglish or any derivative of any language to be acceptable on formal writing assessments that represent entry into the mainstream. It isn't white America; it's job America. Research demonstrates proficiency in writing is required for entrance into that world.

> It remains a social fact that assessments, incompatible though they may be with the linguistic performance and discourse strategies associated with dialects and varieties viewed as substandard, are nonetheless applicable to the objectives and mission of the institutions that employ them. The speech and writing conventions of the community a basic writer seeks to enter cannot be ignored. Or re-engineered, as those familiar with political attempts at language (re)planning can attest (Bernstein *Teaching Developmental Reading*).

I am a writing instructor; therefore, all my students must learn to write. The practical wins out over political. In adjusting best practices of the reading/writing connection, writing as a social act, and grammar instruction to specifically meet the needs of the "basic" writer, I am teaching through the lines of color and ability. Teaching. Empowering. Making a difference. And that benefits the student, and the society, much more than a statement of politics or throwing up my hands ever would. This is a living, breathing legacy. I am not requiring the swimming pool be shallower so these students do not drown. Nor am I throwing them in and saying sink or swim. I'm not the lifeguard; I'm the swim instructor. And while the means may be the backstroke, breaststroke, or just treading water, the goal is still the other side.

CHAPTER 5

Assessment

2 + 3 = ...orange???

IN 1995 THE NCTE (NATIONAL COUNCIL OF Teachers of
English) and CCCC (Conference on College Composition
and Communication) adopted a position statement on writing
assessment that "lists ten assumptions regarding writing
assessment that should be considered when creating new policies
and implementing new classroom practices" ("CCCC Position
Statement" 391). Some of these assumptions, which have been
updated but not changed fundamentally since, assert that
assessment should: be meaningful; drive pedagogy; include multiple
measures; respect language diversity; allow for communication
and feedback; and provide choices for the writer. Yet fifteen years
later, most standardized testing still requires students to sit quietly
and write a final draft in a certain time. Assessment is another
area in which a gap exists between research and practice for
high school English teachers. And yet, the means of assessment
often shapes students' attitudes about writing ("CCCC Position

Statement" 394). They will think of writing as just avoidance of error if multiple choice grammar questions, a component of most formal assessments, are used to evaluate literacy skills instead of the overall purpose, rhetorical choices, and design of a written product. If we want students to understand correctness as part of the context and purpose of lifelong literacy, then we should not subject them to artificial testing environments that do not resemble at all the authentic writing situations they may encounter in their lives. Likewise, if we focus criticism and correction of ELL students' essays primarily on surface level language issues, instead of rhetorical choices and development in all the stages of the writing process, they will not develop as writers. Most of our students use a computer for all of their writing, complete with spell and grammar check, yet on many state assessments they cannot. If we have been assessing their ability to use the computer instead of to edit their own work, they may become frustrated and/or fail the written assessment. Even though the assessment is outdated, incongruent with real-world practices, and ineffective, students still need to pass it. Research indicates that writing is social, and writers learn best when they interact with peers throughout the process, yet on assessments, they may not seek outside help. My professional friends and colleagues seek my assistance several times a week, proofreading and editing memos and articles, even asking about tone or voice or organization. That is part of the real process of writing, which research acknowledges and supports but state assessments do not. How are students to take assessment seriously when it is so obviously not "real world"? Robert Cormier said, "The beautiful part of writing is that you don't have to get it right the first time, unlike, say, a brain surgeon. You can always do it better, find the exact word, the apt phrase, the leaping simile." Yet on these types of assessments, our students often *do* have to be brain surgeons: no second chances, no revision, no talking with colleagues. This encourages a standard of "good enough" but not best. These mixed messages about writing and writing assessment need to be addressed and not ignored in the classroom. Teacher responsibility is two-fold: to prepare students for assessments that gain them entrance into the world of academia and careers; and to prepare them to write *in* that academia and *in* those careers. They are not the same, but preparing them for the latter using research based practices throughout instruction is more likely to ensure success on the assessment; whereas preparing them for the assessment will not allow them the access, knowledge, and motivation they need to write well, period. And as I stated early on in this book, there is another goal for writing instructors – to provide meaningful writing instruction that inspires students to write with and from and for – the heart and soul, and not the test.

State assessments are not used to help students grow as writers. Students usually don't even receive feedback on these tests, that cannot measure potential, or work ethic, or the stages and components of writing and the writing process. Rather, these tests are used in part to evaluate schools and teachers. Students know this, which eliminates all sorts of important criterion for writing well, beginning with authentic purpose and audience. The CCCC's position statement delivers the message that tests should be locally designed and readers should be familiar with the writer's community. My community is an island on the Gulf Coast, where we fish and surf and entertain tourists. A recent assessment included a reading selection about cows. Students here have little to no experience with cows. However, native students were very comfortable with the selection about kayaks. But will all students nationwide be? Another recent reading comprehension assessment, required by all students regardless of nationality, language, or background, repeatedly referenced a "bucking bronco". I had an ELL student who had never been exposed to that term, and was completely at a loss. Research presented here has confirmed that students need opportunities for discussion and feedback during writing. Certainly my student could have asked a classmate what a bucking bronco is, in which case she would have appreciated the figurative language, and been able to more than adequately answer the question. What in the world are we assessing?

The CCCC maintains that assessment should be used to improve learning and drive pedagogy. Currently, research and pedagogy are as far ahead of assessment as classroom teachers are of those creating the assessments. Teachers already know we can and must use assessment to drive learning. And we do: as we identify surface errors, issues of control, organization, creativity, and vocabulary, in our regular informal assessments of student writing, we target specific objectives per assignment for improvement and then assess accordingly. Teachers intuitively let "findings" dictate planning, instruction, and next assessment. Yet "even teachers who recognize and employ the methods used by real writers in working with students can find their best efforts undercut by assessments" (CCCC "Writing Assessment: A Position Statment"). We must ensure that our classroom-generated assessments address both the state goals, and our students' needs - those they recognize and those they cannot yet foresee; then we can lobby for changes at the state level. Assignments like the ones in this text that make the connection between reading and writing, and allow students to interact socially and write for an audience that matters to them, begin to bridge the gap between poor and good assessments. They teach students the real writing process and prepare them to write meaningfully, and correctly, under any conditions. These assignments empower them to revise and edit their own work as they have been instructed in grammar correction, through error analysis, and through meaningful social interaction and exposure to literary models. If students are used to these types of classroom assignments, activities, and informal assessments, their writing will be more than adequate on a formal assessment. Assessing grammar within the context of literacy and communication, and teaching correctness as a valuable component of the writing process and end goals, will motivate and empower students to learn it. Then, they will be able to make better choices on those multiple choice questions and for the timed writing prompts because they will see the larger purpose in what they are being asked to do.

Because of the weight given to "the test," instructors and students mistakenly identify crunch time as test time. On the contrary, the most critical time for students is during the instruction process itself, the rehearsals and not the final performance. State education department officials may not "use multiple measures," "interpret assessment results in ways that are meaningful to students," or "use results from writing assessments to review and (when necessary) revise curriculum" but we as teachers must. "Writing assessment that alienates students from writing is counterproductive." (CCCC "Writing Assessment: A Position Statement"). Regarding state and/or national assessments, one would be wise to claim the serenity prayer, and focus energy on things that *can* be changed, or controlled – and improved – by implementing best practices for writing instruction and assessment, as teachers understand them, in the classroom. In doing so the gap between research and assessment is bridged, and as with all areas of the process, connections are made and the roads converge.

Formal assessments, such as those required on placement tests and entrance exams, are "usually broad in scope and often require students to identify correct writing conventions through contrived items and forced choices" (Scott and Vitale "Informal Assessment of Idea Development"). In fact, in many cases of these multiple choice "revising and editing" questions, none of the choices represents the way the student writer would voice and punctuate the sentence, and some, though technically "incorrect," could be used for emphasis by writers with certain styles. And at times, while a student does not know which choice is correct, he could write the sentence and avoid the error altogether, or would take the initiative to determine the correct way to present the thought if given time to do so, if he cared about the product and audience at all. Yet even though we don't like them, we must prepare students for these types of tests – and to write meaningfully. One method by which teachers can prepare students for both is through informal assessment measures that "use actual student writing samples that are evaluated holistically or with specific skill analysis instruments" (Scott and Vitale "Informal Assessment of Idea Development"). These are the assessments we use to plan and deliver classroom instruction because they are more manageable – both for teachers and students. In addition, they are more realistic, allowing students to define the purpose and audience and create and make their *own* choices. We can teach, practice, and assess writing good thesis sentences in introductions, organizing material into paragraphs, varying sentence structure, using personal narrative or dialogue, or mastering any specific grammatical or rhetorical technique. It does not all have to be done at once. With these smaller assignments, students get more immediate feedback, on a specific goal. This method facilitates mastery - or at least, understanding – and allows instructors to more readily determine which students might need more practice, and in what specific areas, on smaller assignments. Students may be allowed to keep all the small pieces and later have the option to incorporate some of their work – or the ideas in the work – into larger products, for holistic evaluation.

B.J. Scott and Michael Vitale note that teachers have "begun to focus on the higher order cognitive aspects of writing, and have become increasingly aware of the importance of the communicative purpose". They introduce and identify five areas of the concept of "idea development", which they suggest is the most critical aspect of the writing process: audience awareness, content development, organization, cohesiveness, and unity ("Informal Assessment of Idea Development"). These are exactly the areas that qualify excellent writing and areas that should be given more attention in instruction and assessment. "Grading students separately on idea development encourages those who have good ideas but lack mechanical and grammatical skills to express them appropriately" (Scott and Vitale "Informal Assessment of Idea Development"). But if they are assessed on idea development, the ideas must be presented clearly, which requires knowledge and application of grammatical techniques, in a way that matters to students, for their own purposes. I contend even in the stage of idea development we are evaluating holistically – as we have maintained that writing is both stylistic and rhetorical, and grammatical correctness contributes to meaning. In addition, Scott and Vitale claim this technique works well with basic writers, who often are stuck in the "idea" stage because they have trouble "searching memory for generation of content" and "organizing their thoughts". These students with learning disabilities likewise may "fail to include critical elements such as the premise or conclusion of their essays...and they generate a considerable amount of irrelevant or nonfunctional information in their compositions." Working with smaller, manageable parts per assessment initially can allow these students to develop as writers before frustration causes them to give up writing altogether. In addition, students should be clearly informed what the focus of each assignment is. "Such an understanding of what is expected has the potential of making the writing task for students with LD a constructive learning process and a more satisfactory experience" (Scott and Vitale "Informal Assessment of Idea Development"). Separating writing instruction into smaller units, such as idea development, not as isolated building block skills but within the overall projected outcome, helps students understand how various components of the writing process contribute to the end goal, and enables them to view writing within the context of literacy and communication.

Another method of assessment along these same lines is to assign the whole product for the long term, but in sections, or pieces, with due dates along the way. When responding to a literature based prompt for example, students can simply list (prewriting) their reactions, explicate important or relevant quotes, note what their connections to the literature are, and note other connections in literature, politics, the world, or history. Throughout this first component, they would communicate with peers. The next "piece" might be to identify modes, voice, purpose and audience for a written product; then organize all the information into groups, which will become paragraphs. A paragraph may be evaluated for organization, varied sentence structure, unity, and development through examples. It can be assessed grammatically. Students can write a thesis sentence and introduction for a "timed" assessment practice, if this is something that must be achieved. After they draft, they can revise with focus on entire essay cohesiveness and being "connected". At each stage, students can self-assess, receive peer feedback formally and informally, and receive feedback or "grades" from the instructor. This is a type of portfolio assignment through which students are working up to a larger product. Teachers will be able to see "red flags" at points along the process and correct and instruct, allowing for immediate cognition and response and revision. Correctness may be evaluated and strengthened as well during these smaller components, as instructors strive to connect for students that the purpose of language is communication, and correctness strengthens that. It is much better to note that the wiring, fixtures, or paint is wrong before the house is completely built and furnished. But – a builder doesn't start without house plans; thus the holistic approach instead of the linear narrative.

All of this is not to say a teacher should not at times challenge students on an assessment like those required by the state or college entrance exams, *after* the student has been given access, tools, a sound knowledge base, and thus, confidence in his or her ability to communicate through writing. Instructors can, and should, introduce all types of writing situations the student may encounter, and that includes the formal assessment as one genre or set of skills. But there is a difference between an assessment used *during and for instruction,* and assessment to evaluate the efficacy of a teacher or school or a student's readiness to enter a level of academia or profession. For daily and weekly classroom instruction, during the actual learning process, teachers must choose assessment practices that are proven to facilitate that learning.

The contrast between what the research indicates about assessment and what most institutions actually employ is not the only assessment challenge facing writing instructors. One of the biggest differences in English assessment and that of other disciplines (other than the fact that the math teachers are always in the work room drinking coffee with their feet up) is that English is subjective. Forty math graders assess the answer to the algebraic equation and it is wrong or it is right. Check or "X". Forty social studies graders know who the twenty-third president was and it's wrong or it's right. Forty writing instructors read essays describing a single act of kindness that changed a life, and all hell breaks loose. Ten of the graders are grammar nazis and begin immediately circling and underlining and writing code words out in the margins. Ten of the graders read the paper casually, assess a holistic grade, and feel pretty confident that their previous training renders them infallible. Ten of the graders don't like the topic: they don't believe a single act of kindness changes lives in the first place, and they don't like personal writing anyway; they find the topic shallow, and the essays shallower (they ask the grammar nazis if "shallower" is a word). Or they love personal writing, and they write nice, but all completely different, and none particularly constructive, comments on the papers, and show kindness themselves in assigning the grades. The last ten agonize. These graders read the essays laboriously and try to find some positive things and some areas for constructive criticism. They mark some grammar errors, but not too many. They write some notes, then go back and erase (because they do not use red pens, but pencils), and write something different, carefully assigning a grade to the essay as if diagnosing a rare form of cancer. They want to be sure. So while I definitely would *not* call assessment of student writing random, even with a rubric and proper training, it *is* subjective. Just as the writing process is influenced by the writer's own background, personality, beliefs, and experiences, so the assessment process is influenced by the readers'.

I recently participated in a group assessment activity among writing instructors. Two things emerged right away that clearly affected response to the samples of student writing we were given: the ambiguity of intent for the original assignment and how it would be assessed; and the experience and personalities of the graders themselves. I read the portfolio assignments multiple times, but I still couldn't be sure *exactly* what the teacher had in mind that she wanted for her final product, or what had been discussed and taught in class, or the level of the writers in the class. Various responders in this norming exercise interpreted the assignments as differently as the student writers apparently had. Those familiar with portfolio writing looked at progress and tended to grade the essay as part of a whole, while other graders only wanted to evaluate a polished, finished, final product. There were questions about the finished products: did they adequately address the prompt; was the prompt intended to be a guide, or was strict adherence required; how much leeway was acceptable in interpretation and how much was too much? The idea of knowing the students was also introduced for discussion: is it really better to know the students personally and grade progress (even if only in the back of the teacher's mind) or does having anonymous graders, like most exit assessments do, ensure a more valid and fair (what a loaded word) assessment of final product? The student writers themselves interpreted the prompts differently, with some believing they fulfilled the requirements of the assignment when they really did not. For example, one student writer probably thought he had used sources and met the requirement, and one assessor agreed; however, most assessors believed he was asked to analyze *reasons* for the authors' biases and choices, not just report or summarize them. The assigning teacher seemed to focus on the rhetorical, and the student on factual in this case. Regardless, it was clear that the subjective interpretation of the assignment by the writer and the various responders plays a significant role in determining grade. Participating in an activity that required me to interpret another instructor's prompt really drove home to me the importance of making my own assignment goals and expectations clear for students. They should know what is going to be assessed.

Just as writers bring unique backgrounds and experiences and interpretations of prompts to each task, so do those assessing the writing. Experience and personality played a key role in our group norming activity and in how grades were assessed. Teachers are not blank slates; we are real people. As such, we can never be entirely objective about writing. In our initial small group discussion of first drafts, it was interesting that one assessor pinpointed the grammar errors only. I realized that this is what a lot of beginning teachers would do – because it is what they know and are comfortable and confident assessing (editing). After listening to others talk about voice and thesis and organization, she seemed to get ideas of what else to look for and brought a different approach to our second small group discussion. This brought to the forefront that learning to assess writing is like learning to write: it takes lots and lots and lots of practice. All the degrees and knowledge in the world don't make near the difference in quality of teaching – and assessing – that experience does. Assessing dozens or even hundreds of portfolios and essays is not the same as assessing thousands. Knowing the terms and lingo fresh out of college is not the same as understanding what they really mean in the classroom and how they work. One assessor believed a writer's "rhetorical choices were good but he lacked facts." Another argued that was not the case at all; the student had facts from sources; it was the rhetoric that was lacking! If *our* understanding of writing rhetoric and terminology is so different, rendering our grading subjective, imagine the challenge this presents to our students. Experience makes a difference in instruction, and it makes a difference in assessment, just as it makes a difference in writing.

In addition to interpretation of prompt and experience, background and personality contribute to subjectivity. We teach our students that their perspective and voice are often colored by their own experiences. If that is true, are our assessments likewise rendered? Good instructors learn to separate bias and evaluate the written product, but our own political, religious, emotional and cultural backgrounds, and our own experiences with writing or with a particular topic may still come into play during assessment. Even if we are able to evaluate writing and leave out our opinions about content, our personality influences *ideology* about grading. We have all worked with teachers who did not believe in failing a student who "was trying" regardless of final product. Teachers likewise define the "A" paper in vastly different ways. Some prefer to not assign grades at all. In our own group activity, grades ranged from B to F, although most gave C's and D's, which I think is very "safe." But even more interesting – and diverse - than the grades were the reasons behind them, which were completely diverse and incongruent. And I think our lives are reflected in our grading policies. The car of a responder who thinks grammar should not matter at all is likely messy. And the bedroom closet of a grader who believes grammar is the greatest governor, may well be vacuumed and organized by color. The teacher who won't fail any paper ever, probably doesn't discipline her own children much, either. Further opening this can of worms: are conservatives hyper-critical in assessing writing? Are liberals too lenient? Juries are supposed to be fair and impartial also, yet when selecting them, lawyers weigh personality, striking those whom they believe would potentially harm their client or judge him or her harshly. Imagine if students selected their assessors in the same way! Many would select the first year teacher participating in our norming session who scored several papers as "As", and declared upfront that she was grading "holistically" and "not counting off anything for grammar mistakes." Yet some would not want this type of evaluation at all, believing it in fact inhibits their development and quite likely thwarts their long-term goals, communication, and literacy skills. Our personalities and backgrounds come to play in all aspects of life, and assessment is not exempt, and this responding activity reinforced that.

What, then, to do? The assessment challenges loom large, particularly for college entrance, basic writing exit, and high school exit exams. These assessments are scored by individuals who did not create the prompt, do not have the same backgrounds and personalities as each other or as the writers, and do not know the writers or their communities. They will bring all sorts of politics and prejudices with them to the table. They may not "respect language variety and diversity and (assess) writing on the basis of effectiveness for readers . . ." (CCCC "Writing Assessment: A Position Statement"). At the local level, a proactive step is to have activities for staff like the aforementioned, mock grading sessions. Department discussions must take place to ensure that assessment is a true measure of what is taught in the classroom, and that the assessment drives pedagogy. Effective feedback facilitates learning. Instructors must understand what that is, for all writers, and how best to utilize it. We must be informed of and involved with the research regarding assessment and balance our findings with the demands of the state, administration, or other entities to which we owe allegiance, acknowledging at the same time that our most binding allegiance is to the students and the profession. Understanding this, we implement those techniques of writing instruction that research and our own experience have shown are best practices for all writers, not for test takers. We are able to also teach test writing as a genre in our classrooms, as a method, a means, and not an end, thus marrying accountability with meaning and empowering students to write well for all purposes, not sacrificing one for the other – because we know when that sacrifice occurs, we will not let the test – the basic unit of measure, accountability, and transparency in our profession – go; and that which is beautiful about writing, will be lost. Access to the research, such as that presented in this book, is a step in the right direction for meaningful and solid assessment. In shaping our assessments we foster confidence in our students to develop and improve as writers. And effective teaching – and learning – is always our goal.

It is the nature of the discipline: responding to student writing remains subjective, though perhaps it shouldn't be quite as subjective as some would make it. Imagine math teachers having this discussion: "Two plus three is not necessarily five. Or it is, but only if you are from a certain culture and have been exposed to that idea. In *personal* math, it can be seven. Johnny made only a small error and got twelve, so we will give him credit. Melissa got five but her reasoning is flawed; I'm not sure she understood what she was being asked to do." As English teachers, we must be compassionate, and diligent, and assign grades as fairly and consistently as we can when asked to do so. But we must remember the goals of our students and prepare them for success beyond the classroom. In math, a simple addition mistake costs many points – or dollars. In English, a simple sentence structure mistake may be shrugged off. Is that costing our students? In physics class, instructors don't worry about hurting the students' feelings if they have to assign an F. In English we believe somehow we are rejecting the students' very being instead of a mistake on a performance. We flatter ourselves by giving so much credence to our own opinions. We underestimate our students' desire to understand correctness and our own abilities to empower them. Assessments that do not incorporate the research about writing instruction pose a challenge, but teachers may be encouraged that best practices for instruction are not incongruent with good results on formal assessments. The subjectivity demonstrated in the aforementioned norming activity remains one of the field's Achilles heels. Nevertheless, even in writing assessments, two plus three is not orange.

CONCLUSION

The Difference

"You can't wait for inspiration, you have to go after it with a club." –Jack London

BUSINESSES BASE PLANS TO INCREASE PRODUCTIVITY ON research. Theory and research ought to inform the practice of writing instruction as well. Accountability is not a bad thing. But it emphasizes what will be tested – not what must be taught, and learned. That is up to the classroom teacher. "When writing teachers first walk into classrooms, they should already know and practice good composition. However, much as in doctoring, learning to teach well is a lifetime process, and lifetime professional development is the key to successful practice. Students deserve no less"("NCTE Beliefs About the Teaching of Writing"). What teachers believe about writing instruction may not be entirely wrong. But it may not be *all there is* to know, the very best we can offer every student, in every situation, for every occasion. Even though my own students always scored high on state assessments, college entrance tests, and advanced placement tests, when I began to apply the ideas and theories from my own reading and research to the classroom, there was obvious improvement in the depth, breadth, and quality of my students' writing. This research should give teachers pause.

English teachers have to see beyond this idea of polarization in writing instruction, by making connections, and going beyond limits and restrictions of artificial, uniform standards set for our students. The roads and goals of the state and those of writing instructors are not divergent at all: we can and must empower our students through access, means, and motivation, to take both roads, and enjoy them. To be truly effective, writing teachers must apply curricular strategies that utilize the reading-writing connection, such as purposefully selecting reading material and using the language of literary texts to teach recognition, appreciation, and application of grammatical, stylistic and rhetorical choices. We must provide students with professional and student examples of the types of writing that they are assigned to produce, giving purpose and meaning to both what they read and what they write. We should recognize and give credence to the social aspect of writing, helping students articulate and make meaning throughout the process, beyond a timed, formulaic product, for an audience other than the teacher. This may begin as simply as incorporating group discussion about a prompt, or a good revision activity. We must instruct in the correctness of style with an eye on purpose, helping all students not to be limited by their voice in the world, but to improve their platform and presentation enough that the world will acknowledge that voice, regardless of background, home language, or disability. When the ELL, mainstreamed, or "basic" writers enter our classrooms they deserve the same keys of opportunity and access to the many kingdoms of literacy. These can be provided through specific methods of instruction within best practices for all students, and not through political fervor, or excuses. When the skill and drill worksheets don't seem to be working – or when a teacher is just bored and tired of teaching grammar the same way, with the same results – he or she may pause, and wonder if there are practical, more effective methods out there for providing some kind of authentic engagement and relevance for the students. Finally, teachers must balance what research indicates about assessment with what is mandated by the school or state. The powers that design and implement standardized tests, and hand down teacher directives and salaries, may not be aware of what works best for students, but teachers do not have to be so hindered, particularly during the instruction process, when we are not testing but teaching, and when our students' beliefs and attitudes about writing are formed.

The pause may come when, like me, instructors realize with disgust that in response to the pendulum, politics, or pressures of accountability, curricular demands, and time, they have inadvertently contributed to a wrong mentality of "good enough", for both our own instruction and the actual writing the students produce, propelling more and more students to the minimum standards, and less and less to greatness. We may all be doing the limbo, shimmying under the bar, until we finally ask ourselves: how low can we go? Deep down, we aren't satisfied; we don't want to place blame or make excuses. We want to find better ways of teaching the skills we know our student writers need to have. The pause for some may come when reading this book, as it did for me when preparing to write it.

Instructors in any classroom must consider the content and methods on current syllabi and in the required curriculum and determine if they do in fact represent the very best practices – and how do we know, if we don't know what else is out there? If teachers do not stay abreast of current research, we are vulnerable to traditional paradigms and lore, and we limit ourselves to prior knowledge in much the same way we limit our students. Just as our students fail to connect correctness with composition, and writing with communication, we fail to connect research with practice, and meaningful instruction with assessment demands. We are picked up, swung, or bounced by the pendulum of current politics, trends, or accountability measures, because we aren't on solid ground to begin with, or we were, and just forgot. We may not be in Kansas anymore, but we don't have to be in the wind, either. Instructors need the same exposure and access to improvement that our students do. To inspire our students, we first must be inspired.

We can teach meaningful writing in an age of testing. If we apply research to practice in our classrooms, learning experiences of all students will be enhanced, the tests will not be daunting, and the soul of writing will not be lost. Writing instructors can make "the classroom itself a bridge to the world outside; assignments become a way for students to better understand their own lives, as well as academic expectations" (Adler-Kassner and Harrington 60). These ideas don't challenge traditional notions of literacy as much as they challenge teachers to continue to seek the best for their students. In teaching our students to write well for all purposes, we are teaching them to write for the test. The reverse, however, just isn't true. Two roads diverged and I took both; and that has made the difference.

WORKS CITED

Adler-Kassner, Linda and Gregory R. Glau. The Bedford Bibliography For Teachers of Basic Writing. Second Edition. New York: Bedford/St. Martin's, 2005.

Adler-Kassner, Linda and Susanmarie Harrington. Basic Writing as a Political Act: Public Conversations About Writing and Literacies. New Jersey: Hampton Press, Inc., 2002.

Agnew, Eleanor and Margaret McLaughlin. "Those Crazy Gates and How They Swing: Tracking the System That Tracks African-American Students." Mainstreaming Basic Writers: Politics and Pedagogies of Access. Ed. Gerri McNenny. Lawrence Erlbaum Associates: Mahwah, NJ: 2001.

Austen, Jane. Pride and Prejudice. London: British Books LTD.

Barbery, Muriel. The Elegance of the Hedgehog. New York: Europa Editions, 2008.

"Basic Writing: Teachers' Perspectives." Teaching Developmental Writing: Background Readings. 3rd Ed. Ed. Susan Naomi Bernstein. Boston: Bedford/St. Martin's, 2007: 1.

Bernstein, Susan Naomi. "The Impact of State-Mandated Testing on Basic Writing." Teaching Basic Writing.

McGraw-Hill, 2003. http://www.mhhe.com/socscience/
english/tbw/berstein/bernsteinModule.htm

Bernstein, Susan Naomi, Ed. (2004). Teaching Developmental
Reading: Background Readings. (Second Edition).
Boston, New York: Bedford/St. Martin's.

Bosley, Cindy. "How I Lost the Junior Miss Pageant." The
Composition of Everyday Life: A Guide to Writing. Eds.
John Mauk and John Metz. Wadsworth Publishing:
USA, 2003.

"CCCC Position Statement." Teaching Developmental Writing:
Background Readings. 3rd Ed. Ed Susan Naomi
Bernstein. Boston: Bedford/St. Martin's, 2007: 390-399.

"CCCC Statement on Second Language Writing and Writers."
CCCC. Revised Nov. 2009. http://www.ncte.org/cccc/
resources/positions/secondlangwriting

CCCC. "Writing Assessment: A Position Statement." www.ncte.
org/cccc Crisco, Virginia. "Rethinking Language and
Culture on the Institutional Borderland." *Journal of Basic
Writing.* V. 23. Spring 2004: 39-63.

Dickson, Marcia. "Learning to Read/Learning to Write."
Journal of Basic Writing. Eds. Linda Adler-Kassner and
Gregory R. Glau. Vol. 1. Summer 1999.

Dunning, S., & Stafford, W. (1992). Found and headline
poems. In *Getting the knack: 20 poetry writing exercises*
(pp.3-23). Urbana, IL. NCTE.

Faulkner, William. "Barn Burning." Backpack Literature: An
Introduction to Fiction, Poetry, Drama, and Writing.
Eds. X.J. Kennedy and Dana Gioia. New York: Pearson-
Longman, 2008. 124-138.

Fu, Danling; Shelton, Nancy R. "Including Students with Special Needs in a Writing Workshop". *Language Arts*. 01 Mar 2007: 325. *eLibrary*. Web. 22 Jan 2010.

Goen-Salter, Sugie. "Integrated Reading and Writing: A Response to the Basic Writing 'Crisis.'" Teaching Basic Writing Online. McGraw-Hill, 2004. Http://www.mhhe.com/ socscience/english/tbw/goen/goen_module.html

Graff, Gerald and Cathy Birkenstein. They Say I Say: The Moves That Matter in Academic Writing. New York: W. W. Norton and Co., Inc, 2006.

Hagemann, Julie Ann. "Balancing content and form in the writing workshop". *English Journal*. 01 Jan 2003: 73. *eLibrary*. Web. 22 Jan 2010.

Hartman, Beth and Elaine Tarone. "From Preparation for College Writing." Teaching Developmental Writing: Background Readings. 3rd Ed. Ed. Susan Naomi Bernstein. Boston: Bedford/St. Martin's, 2007: 381-389.

Hartwell, Patrick. "Grammar, Grammars, and the Teaching of Grammar." *College English*. Vol. 47. No. 2. Feb. 1985: 105-127.

Hemingway, Ernest. "A Clean, Well-Lighted Place." Backpack Literature: An Introduction to Fiction, Poetry, Drama, and Writing. Eds. X.J. Kennedy and Dana Gioia. New York: Pearson-Longman, 2008.

Jordan, June. "Nobody Mean More to Me than You and the Future Life of Willie Jordan." *Harvard Educational Review*. v. 58. Aug. 1988: 363-374.

King, Stephen. On Writing: A Memoir of the Craft. New York: Simon & Schuster, Inc., 2000.

Lehman College. "Resources for Faculty – Handling Surface Errors in Student Writing." http://www.lehman.edu/lehman/wac/facultyresources_surface_error.html

Levin, Amy. "Goals and Philosophies of High School Writing Centers." The High School Writing Center: Establishing and Maintaining One. Ed. Pamela B. Farrell. USA: NCTE, 1989: 23-29.

McNenny, Gerri, Ed. Basic Writers: Politics and Pedagogies of Access. New Jersey: Lawrence Erlbaum Associates, 2001.

Mori, Kyoko. "School." *The Language of Composition: Reading, Writing, Rhetoric.* Eds. Renee H. Shea, Lawrence Scanlon, and Robin Dissin Aufses. New York: Bedford/St. Martin's, 2008. 130-142.

"NCTE Beliefs about the Teaching of Writing." National Council of Teachers of English. 1998-2007. http://www.ncte.org/about/over/positions/category/write/118876.htm

"NCTE Position Paper on the Role of the English Teacher in Educating English Language Learners (ELLs)." NCTE ELL Task Force. April 2006. http://www.ncte.org/positions/statements/teacherseducatingell

Neuleib, Janice and Irene Brosnahan. "Teacher Grammar to Writers." Teaching Developmental Writing: Background Readings. 3rd Ed. Ed. Susan Naomi Bernstein. Boston: Bedford/St. Martin's, 2007: 145-153.

Prose, Francine. "I Know Why the Caged Bird Cannot Read: How American High School Students Learn to Loathe Literature." The Language of Composition: Reading, Writing, Rhetoric. Eds. Renee H. Shea, Lawrence Scanlon, and Robin Dissin Aufses. New York: Bedford/St. Martin's, 2008. 89-99.

Prose, Francine. <u>Reading Like a Writer: A Guide for People Who Love Books and For Those Who Want to Write Them.</u> New York: HarperCollins, 2006.

Reynolds, Thomas J; Bruch, Patrick L. "Curriculum and affect: A participatory developmental writing approach". *Journal of Developmental Education*. 01 Jan 2002: 12. *eLibrary*. Web. 22 Jan 2010.

Rich, Adrienne. 1972. "Teaching Language in Open Admissions." In Engel, Monroe. (Ed.) 1973. <u>The Uses of Literature.</u> Cambridge, MA: Harvard University.

Scott, B.J; Vatale, Michael R. "Informal Assessment of Idea Development in Written Expression: A Tool for Classroom Use." *Preventing School Failure* 2 (2000): 67. eLibrary. Web. 09 Feb 2010.

Scott, B.J; Vitale, Michael R. "Teaching the writing process to students with LD". *Intervention in School & Clinic* 4(2003):220. *eLibrary*. Web. 22 Jan 2010.

Shaughnessy, Mina. "Some New Approaches toward Teaching." <u>Teaching Developmental Writing: Background Readings.</u> 3rd Ed. Ed. Susan Naomi Bernstein. Boston: Bedford/St. Martin's, 2007: 2-13.

Shor, Ira. "Errors and Economics: Inequality Breeds Remediation." <u>Mainstreaming Basic Writers: Politics and Pedagogies of Access.</u> Ed. Gerri McNenny. New Jersey: Lawrence Erlbaum Associates, 2001: 29-54.

Shosh, Joseph M; Zales, Charlotte Rappe. "Daring to Teach Writing Authentically, K-12 and Beyond". *English Journal*. 01 Nov 2005: 77. *eLibrary*. Web. 22 Jan 2010.

Singer, Marti. "Moving the Margins." <u>Mainstreaming Basic Writing: Politics and Pedagogies of Access.</u> Ed. Gerri

McNenny. New Jersey: Lawrence Erlbaum Associates, 2001: 101-118.

Steinbeck, John. <u>The Grapes of Wrath.</u> New York: Penguin Group, 2002.

Tannen, Deborah. "Sex, Lies and Conversation: Why Is It So Hard for Men and Women to Talk to Each Other?" *The Washington Post.* June 24, 1990.

Thurston, Kay. "Mitigating Barriers to Navajo Students' Success in English Courses." *Teaching English in the Two-Year College.* V. 26. Sept. 1998 (29-38).

Uehling, Karen S. "Teaching About Language." <u>http://www.mhhe.com/socscience/english/tbw/pt/uehling/teaching_about_language.htm</u>

VanDeWeghe, Rick. "Research Matters". *English Journal.* 01 Mar 2007: 94. *eLibrary.* Web. 22 Jan 2010.

White, Linda Feldmeier. "Learning Disability, Pedagogies, and Public Discourse." *College Composition and Communication*, Vol. 53, No. 4 (Jun., 2002), pp. 705-738. NCTE.

CPSIA information can be obtained
at www.ICGtesting.com
Printed in the USA
FFOW02n0534300518
46962212-49215FF